Costume in Motion

Costume in Motion is a guide to all stages of the collaboration process between costume designers and choreographers, documenting a wide range of approaches to the creation of a dance piece.

Featuring interviews with a diverse selection of over 40 choreographers and designers, in-depth case studies of works by leading dance companies, and stunning original photography, the book explores the particular challenges and creative opportunities of designing for the body in motion. Filled with examples of successful collaborations in contemporary and modern dance, as well as a wide range of other styles, *Costume in Motion* provides costume designers and choreographers with a greater understanding of the field from the other's perspective.

The book is designed to be part of the curriculum for an undergraduate or graduate level course in costume design or choreography, and it can also be an enriching read for artists at any stage of their careers wishing to hone their collaboration skills in dance.

E. Shura Pollatsek is a professional costume designer for stage and screen, a Professor of Costume Design and Technology at WKU, and an award-winning author of many nationally published articles. She is also the author of the book *Unbuttoned: The Art and Artists of Theatrical Costume Design*, another collaboration with Mitchell D. Wilson. She has designed costumes for theater and dance performances across the US and internationally, and for National PBS television and Showtime. During a decade based in New York City, she worked for Off-Broadway and Broadway productions, the Metropolitan Opera, and at many leading regional theaters.

Mitchell D. Wilson is a National Press Photographer of the Year winner who travels the world capturing time and place in stills and motion. His work has also been recognized with Primetime Emmys, both the DuPont Columbia Award and the Peabody for Excellence in Broadcast Journalism, two International Documentary Association Awards for Best Documentary Series, and many others. He began his career as a Combat Cameraman and underwater photographer in the elite Combat Camera Group of the US Navy.

Ensemble dancers of Contra-Tiempo perform *joyUS justUS* (for more detail see Case Study #1)

Costume in Motion

A Guide to Collaboration for Costume Design and Choreography

E. Shura Pollatsek

Photography by Mitchell D. Wilson

Routledge
Taylor & Francis Group

NEW YORK AND LONDON

First published 2021
by Routledge
605 Third Avenue, New York, NY 10017

and by Routledge
2 Park Square, Milton Park, Abingdon, Oxon, OX14 4RN

Routledge is an imprint of the Taylor & Francis Group, an informa business

© 2021 Taylor & Francis

Photography © 2021 Mitchell D. Wilson

Library of Congress Cataloging-in-Publication Data
Names: Pollatsek, E. Shura, author. | Wilson, Mitchell D., photographer.
Title: Costume in motion : a guide to collaboration for costume design and
    choreography / E. Shura Pollatsek ; photography by Mitchell D. Wilson.
Description: New York, NY : Routledge, 2021. | Includes bibliographical
    references and index.
Identifiers: LCCN 2020046793 (print) | LCCN 2020046794 (ebook) |
    ISBN 9780815366881 (hardback) | ISBN 9780815366874 (paperback) |
    ISBN 9781351258524 (ebook)
Subjects: LCSH: Costume design. | Dance costume. | Choreography.
Classification: LCC PN2067 .P646 2021 (print) | LCC PN2067 (ebook) | DDC
    792.02/6—dc23
LC record available at https://lccn.loc.gov/2020046793
LC ebook record available at https://lccn.loc.gov/2020046794

ISBN 13: 978-0-8153-6688-1 (hbk)
ISBN 13: 978-0-8153-6687-4 (pbk)
ISBN 13: 978-1-351-25852-4 (ebk)

Typeset in ITC Slimbach Std
by Apex CoVantage, LLC

Contents

Acknowledgments

I am finishing this book in the summer of 2020, as the COVID-19 epidemic has closed nearly all live events. As I rephrase descriptions of stage artistry, I am constantly reminded of how much I value, and previously took for granted, the day-to-day interaction and side-by-side work of the performing arts. I hope that the stories in this book prove useful and inspiring to artists in dance and costume who seek new ways to make art from a distance, and also as we return to closer collaborations in the future.

I want to thank all of the designers and choreographers interviewed for this book who so generously shared their stories, artistry and expertise. While a few were longtime colleagues, most were complete strangers who agreed to give their time to the project. And, I am especially grateful to the seven dance companies that let us visit them and take photographs. They proved to be gracious hosts, even during the whirlwind of dress rehearsals.

I am indebted to those who gave both personal and professional support during the development, writing and completion of this book: Potter College of Arts and Letters and the WKU Office of Research and Sponsored Programs that funded much of the travel required to research the book; David Young and the rest of my colleagues in the WKU Department of Theatre and Dance for their encouragement; the editors and staff at Routledge who helped us to shape the manuscript; family and friends who cheered us and provided welcome distractions.

I especially want to thank my collaborator: my husband Mitch Wilson. Your photography never ceases to amaze me with its unexpected details and gorgeous composition. Thank you for trekking with me to random cities around the country, where you mainly got to see the inside of darkened auditoriums, and for putting up with me spending hours hiding in my office staring at a computer.

Finally, none of this would have been possible without my parents, Harriet and Sandy. They instilled in me a love of creativity, craftsmanship and artistic expression. I am grateful for how much exposure I had at an early age to all aspects of the arts—visiting museums around the world, music lessons, painting storefront murals, and seeing *The Nutcracker* every December, most years in person.

E. Shura Pollatsek is the author of the book *Unbuttoned: The Art and Artists of Theatrical Costume Design*, also a collaboration with Mitch Wilson, and has published numerous articles in national magazines, one of which won the Herbert Greggs Merit Award.

Shura is a versatile costume designer whose work spans theater, dance, opera, film and television. She designed costumes for Off Broadway venues including the Pearl Theatre, HERE and the Storm Theatre. Dance designs include *Halcyon* with Christopher K. Morgan & Artists and *Thirst*, performed at the Kennedy Center and on international tours by CityDance Ensemble. For national television, she designed costumes for *The Duel* and *Woodrow Wilson* on PBS' The American Experience, and *The Kingdom of David* and *Andrew Jackson*, also for National PBS. Shura has been assistant costume designer for Broadway, including *Thoroughly Modern Millie* and *All Shook Up*, and for the Metropolitan Opera.

She holds an MFA in Costume Design from New York University's Tisch School of the Arts and is a proud member of United Scenic Artists Local 829. After many years as a freelance artist, she is now based in Kentucky, where she is Professor of Costume Design and Technology at Western Kentucky University.

Mitchell D. Wilson is well-known for cinematic eloquence, impressionistic historical re-creations and striking juxtaposition of photojournalism and visual metaphor. He has traveled the world capturing time and place in stills and motion. His striking photos are collected in books, and along with multimedia pieces, have also been exhibited in galleries. Favorite projects include *Andrew Jackson: Good, Evil and the Presidency* and the four-hour PBS series *The New Heroes*, hosted by Robert Redford. His cinematography for the series was nominated for a National Emmy award. Other projects include *The Kingdom of David, When Worlds Collide* about the origins of Hispanic culture, *The Meth Epidemic* for Frontline and the four-hour PBS history of aviation project *Chasing the Sun*. He served as Co-Director and Cinematographer for the three-hour Woodrow Wilson presidential special, and *The Duel*, both for The American Experience, PBS' preeminent history series.

His impressive list of PBS credits includes the eight-hour, award-winning series *The Great War and the Shaping of the Twentieth Century*. His creative talents have also been widely showcased on ABC, NBC, CBS and HBO. A National Press Photographer of the Year winner, his work has also been recognized with Primetime Emmys, the DuPont Columbia Award and the Peabody for Excellence in Broadcast Journalism, two International Documentary Association Awards for Best Documentary Series, the Producers Guild of America Kodak Vision Award, the Ohio State Award, the Indian Film Festival Audience Choice award, Press Club honors from UP and API and multiple Los Angeles Emmys and Los Angeles Press Club Awards. He began his career as a combat cameraman and underwater photographer in the elite Combat Camera Group of the US Navy. He is also a member of the Directors Guild of America.

For more information, please visit shuracostumedesign.com and mitchelldwilson.com

Aubrey Hyde and Lauren Terry from Nashville Ballet perform *The Four Seasons* choreographed by Paul Vasterling with costume design by David Heuvel)

CHOREOGRAPHERS

Kyle Abraham

In addition to choreography for his company, Abraham in Motion, which performs nationally and internationally, Abraham has choreographed for companies including Alvin Ailey American Dance Theater, American Ballet Theater, Hubbard Street Dance Chicago, New York City Ballet and Paul Taylor American Modern Dance Company. Honors include the Doris Duke Artist Award, a MacArthur Fellowship and a Princess Grace Statue award.

Ana Maria Alvarez

Artistic Director Alvarez founded CONTRA-TIEMPO Urban Latin Dance Theater in 2005. The company views community engagement as an integral part of their artistic production and they have partnerships with many neighborhoods in South LA. Her choreography has been performed nationally and internationally at venues including Jacob's Pillow, Lincoln Center, Skirball Cultural Center and Teatro Favorito in Cuba. Honors include NEFA National Dance Project and National Association of Latino Arts and Cultures.

Bryan Arias

Arias is the founder of the ARIAS company and has also choreographed for Ballet Theater Basel, the Julliard School, Netherlands Dance Theater 2 and the Paul Taylor Company. Honors include First Place and Audience Choice awards at the Sixth Copenhagen International Choreography Competition, the Princess Grace Choreography Fellowship Award and the Jacob's Pillow Fellowship Award.

Joy Bollinger

Bollinger is Artistic Director of Bruce Wood Dance. She has worked with the company for over 16 years, first as a dancer, and then as rehearsal director and répétiteur of the company, restaging works of the founder Bruce Wood. She has choreographed several works for Bruce Wood Dance and also for Dallas Black Dance Theatre and Texas Christian University.

Jack Ferver

Ferver's interdisciplinary performance works have been presented in New York at venues including New York Live Arts, the New Museum, the Kitchen, PS 122 and also at Théâtre de Vanves in France. He is a writer, choreographer and director. Honors include residencies and fellowships with Baryshnikov Arts Center, Abrons Art Center and the Foundation for Contemporary Arts Grant.

Ingri Fiksdal

Fiksdal is an Oslo-based choreographer, specializing in affective choreography. Her works have toured in her native Norway and around Europe, as well as the United States and China. She has been chosen for funding by the Norwegian Arts Council and apap-Performing Europe 2020.

Liz Gerring

Gerring founded the Liz Gerring Dance Company in 1998. She presents her work in New York City and internationally at venues including Jacob's Pillow, Montclair State and the Joyce Theater. Honors include City Center Choreographic Fellowship, the Jacob's Pillow Prize and the Cage-Cunningham Fellowship from the Baryshnikov Arts Center.

Nicole Haskins

A company member of Smuin Contemporary American Ballet, Haskins also serves as Resident Choreographer of Mid-Columbia Ballet. She has choreographed for companies including Oregon Ballet Theater, Richmond Ballet, Sacramento Ballet and Smuin Ballet. Honors include being a winner of Oregon Ballet Theatre's Choreography XX competition, and the New York Choreographic Institute's Fellowship Grant and Commission Initiative.

xii About the Artists Interviewed

Roni Koresh

Koresh founded Koresh Dance Company in 1991, and blends ballet, modern and jazz into his works. The company performs in their Philadelphia home, and tours nationally and internationally, including to Mexico, Spain, South Korea and Koresh's native Israel. He has been supported by groups including the Pew Charitable Trusts, the National Endowment for the Arts and the Jerome Robins foundation.

Trey McIntyre

McIntyre, founder of the Trey McIntyre Project, has also worked for more than 25 years as a freelance choreographer for companies including Stuttgart Ballet, American Ballet Theatre, Hubbard Street Dance Chicago and BalletX. Honors include a Choo San Goh Award for Choreography and a Lifetime Achievement Award from the National Society of Arts and Letters and he is a United States Artists Fellow. McIntyre is also a photographer, published in numerous newspapers and magazines.

Ray Mercer

Mercer, a 16-year member of the cast of *The Lion King*, has choreographed for companies including Ailey II, Giordano Dance Chicago, Dallas Black Dance Theatre and Pensacola Ballet. Honors include seven Best Onstage Presentation awards for Broadway Cares/Equity Fights AIDS Gypsy of the Year competition, Joffrey Ballet's Choreographers of Color Award and being named a Capezio Ace Awards finalist.

Christopher K. Morgan

Morgan is Artistic and Executive Director of Christopher K. Morgan & Artists in Washington, DC. After five years as Choreographer in Residence at CityDance, he founded CKM&A in 2011, and his work has been performed throughout the US and internationally. Honors include the Dance Metro DC Award for Outstanding New Work, the NPN Creation Fund Award and the NEFA National Dance Project Production Grant.

Anuradha Nehru

Nehru is Artistic Director of Kalanidhi Dance, which she founded in 1991. A dancer, choreographer and teacher of the Kuchipudi style of Indian classical dance, she choreographs for Kalanidhi Dance, which has performed around the US and internationally. She also has collaborated with Opera Lafayette on three productions. Honors include receiving the Master/Apprentice Grant from the Maryland State Arts Council and the Montgomery County Executive's Outstanding Artist Award.

Ranee Ramaswamy

Ramaswamy founded Ragamala Dance Company in 1992 and is Co-Artistic Director, Choreographer and Principal Dancer. The company performs the classical Indian style Bharatanatyam merged with a Western aesthetic. Her choreography has been commissioned by companies including Lincoln Center, Walker Art Center and the Arts Center at NYU Abu Dhabi. Honors include a Doris Duke Artist Award and a United States Artists Fellowship, and she serves on the National Council on the Arts.

Dwight Rhoden

Rhoden is Founding Artistic Director/Resident Choreographer of Complexions Contemporary Ballet. Since 1994, he has choreographed over 80 ballets for Complexions, and also for companies including Alvin Ailey American Dance Theater, the Joffrey Ballet and the San Francisco Ballet. His work has been performed internationally on five continents. Honors include the New York Foundation for the Arts Award, the 2001 Choo San Goh Award for Choreography and the Ailey School's Apex Award.

Jenny Rocha

Rocha, Artistic Director of Rocha Dance Theater, is a choreographer, dancer and costume designer. She is also the director of The Painted Ladies, a cabaret group. Her choreography has been presented at venues including the Philadelphia Museum of Art, the Boston Center for the Arts, Danspace Project and La MaMa. Honors include the Puffin Foundation Grant, Galapagos Art Space Residency, and an Innovation Grant from the US Embassy in Lisbon.

Iddrisu Saaka

Saaka is a West African dance teacher, dancer, drummer and choreographer who has choreographed and performed at venues including the World Festival of Sacred Music, the International Festival of Masks, the Skirball Center, Royce Hall, the Fowler Museum, Dance Arts Academy, Debbie Allen Dance Academy, El Portal Forum Theatre and the Music Center in Los Angeles. He also released *Gonja Dreams*, an album of original music that combines African and Western musical styles.

Amy Seiwert

Seiwert is Artistic Director of Sacramento Ballet and founder of Amy Seiwert's Imagery. She was Choreographer in Residence at Smuin Ballet, and also has choreographed for companies including Washington Ballet, Colorado Ballet, American Repertory Ballet and AXIS Dance. Honors include the New York Choreography Institute, a Bay Area IZZIE award for Outstanding Choreography and a "Goldie" from the *San Francisco Bay Guardian*.

Jody Sperling

Sperling is Founder and Artistic Director of Time Lapse Dance, which has performed since 2000 throughout the US and internationally. Her works have been featured in the repertory of the Netherlands' Introdans ensemble and performed by Ice Theatre of New York. Honors include nomination for a World Choreography Award for her work on *The Dancer*, a film about Loie Fuller that premiered at the Cannes Film Festival.

Paul Vasterling

Vasterling has been Artistic Director of Nashville Ballet since 1998. He has created over 40 works for the company. His work has been performed at the Kennedy Center, the Chautauqua Institution, and abroad. His choreography has also been staged by companies nationally and internationally. Honors include fellowships at Virginia Center for the Creative Arts and the Center for Ballet and the Arts at New York University.

Septime Webre

Webre is currently Artistic Director of Hong Kong Ballet, after serving as Artistic Director of the Washington Ballet for 17 years and the American Repertory Ballet for six. His choreography has been performed by companies including Pacific Northwest Ballet, Les Grands Ballets Canadiens, Colorado Ballet, Ballet West and Ballet Concierto de Puerto Rico. He has served on the board of Dance/USA and his work has received numerous honors, grants and awards.

Gundija Zandersona

Zandersona is a freelance contemporary dancer and choreographer based in Cardiff, Wales. Much of her training has focused on improvisation for performance and contact improvisation. She was commissioned by the University of South Wales to choreograph two contemporary dance works and had a residency at National Dance Company Wales.

COSTUME DESIGNERS

Zepur Agopyan

Agopyan is a set and costume designer based in Wales. She works in film, theater and dance. She was an award-winner for Costume Design at the World Stage Design Exhibition 2017 in Taipei.

John Ahrens

Ahrens is the longtime resident costume designer of Bruce Wood Dance. He has also designed costumes for Dallas Ballet, Fort Worth Ballet, Ballet Austin and Dancers Unlimited. He began his career in New York City working with Betty Williams for companies such as Martha Graham, José Limón, Merce Cunningham and Paul Taylor.

L'Amour Ameer (L'Amour)

L'Amour is the Costume Designer and Wardrobe Manager, and a former dancer, for Dayton Contemporary Dance Company. He is also a fashion designer with an haute couture line. His work has been featured in *Bride Noir*, *Ebony*, *Jet* and *Urban Flava*.

Charlese Antoinette

Antoinette is a stylist, costume designer and jewelry designer. Recent costume designs for the screen include *Raising Dion*, *See You Yesterday*, *Astronomy Club* and *Sprinter*. She has designed films that premiered at Sundance, Tribeca Film Festival and SXSW. Her jewelry has been worn by Beyoncé and Zoë Kravitz and featured in Rihanna's music videos.

Elena Comendador

Comendador has designed costumes for companies including Ailey II, Colorado Ballet, Complexions Contemporary Ballet, Montgomery Ballet, Philadanco and the Limón Dance Company. A former dancer, Comendador was on the ballet faculty of the Ailey School and now is Assistant Professor of Dance at Marymount Manhattan College.

Christine Darch

Darch designs costumes primarily for dance, and has collaborated with choreographers including Julia Adam, Amy Seiwert, James Kudelka, Dwight Rhoden and Matthew Neenan. Her designs have been performed by companies including Atlanta Ballet, Houston Ballet, Oregon Ballet Theatre and San Francisco Ballet. She also designs scenery and has designed costume and sets for films shown at the Sundance Festival.

David Heuvel

Heuvel is the Director of Costume Production at Ballet West. He is Principal Guest Costume Designer for Carolina Ballet, and has also designed for companies including Richmond Ballet, Ballet Du Nord, Singapore Ballet, Oregon Ballet Theatre and Ballet West. He has received the Utah Governor's Artist Award for Visual Arts.

Branimira Ivanova

Ivanovna has designed costumes for companies including Hubbard Street Dance Chicago, Giordano Dance Chicago, Aspen Santa Fe Ballet, Pacific Northwest Ballet, the Portuguese National Ballet and Gauthier Dance in Germany. She also designs for theater, has a clothing company, and won a Certificate of Excellence in Theater Design from USITT and a Jeff Award (Equity Wing) for Best Costume Design.

Holly Hynes

Hynes has designed over 250 ballets for companies around the world, including American Ballet Theatre, Bolshoi Ballet, National Ballet of Canada, La Scala Ballet, Ballet de l'Opéra de Paris and many others. She is also the resident costume designer for the Suzanne Farrell Ballet in Washington, DC. She was Director of Costumes for New York City Ballet for 21 years and designed more than 70 ballets there. She also serves as a consultant for recreations of original designs for Balanchine and Robbins ballet costumes. Hynes is a recipient of the TDF/Irene Sharaff Lifetime Achievement Award in Costume Design.

Mary Jo Mecca

Mecca has designed for choreographers including Rebecca Lazier, Zvi Gotheiner, Rashaun Mitchell, Susan Marshall and Brian Brooks. She studied couture design with Miss Alice Sapho of Paris and New York. Mecca also designs for the Theatre/Dance Department at Princeton University.

Emily Morgan

Morgan is Costume Director of Richmond Ballet. She has designed for choreographers including Nicole Haskins, Katarzyna Skarpetowska, Tom Mattingly and Edgar Zendejas.

Reid & Harriet Design

Reid Bartelme and Harriet Jung formed Reid & Harriet Design in 2011. They have designed costumes for choreographers including Justin Peck, Pontus Lidberg, Marcelo Gomes, Pam Tanowitz, Emery LeCrone, Kyle Abraham, Mauro Bigonzetti, and Doug Varone. They have worked at American Ballet Theater, New York City Ballet, Miami City Ballet, Pacific Northwest Ballet, and many others.

Robin Shane

Shane is a costume designer primarily for theater. Her work has been seen at theaters including Berkeley Repertory Theater, Theatre Exile, Philadelphia Artist's Collective, EgoPo, Passage Theater and the Shakespeare Theater of New Jersey. She is Assistant Professor of Costume Design at Rider University.

Liz Vandal

Vandal has designed for dance companies including Compagnie Marie Chouinard, Les Grands Ballets Canadiens de Montréal, le Ballet National du Canada, Washington Ballet, Stuttgart Ballet, Hong Kong Ballet and l'Opéra de Paris. She has also designed for circus including *OVO* for Cirque du Soleil, for film and a tour for the Backstreet Boys.

Henrik Vibskov

Vibskov is a Danish fashion designer and costume designer for opera, theater and dance who also presents solo exhibits of his work in art museums. He has designed costumes for many companies around the world, including the Royal Swedish Ballet, the Royal Norwegian Ballet and Phantom Limp at Brooklyn Academy of Music. He also designed *Medúlla* by Björk. Among the many awards for his work are the Royal Thorvald Bindesbøll Medal, the Jury Prize at the Danish Fashion Awards, and the Söderberg Prize.

Melanie Watnick

Watnick is a designer for theater and dance. She has designed for dance companies including BalletX, Complexions Contemporary Ballet, Singapore Dance Theatre and Malashock Dance. Her theatre design includes Juilliard, Seattle Repertory and San Diego Repertory Theatre. She is Adjunct Professor at Pepperdine University, and was previously on the faculty at University of California Irvine.

Sandra Woodall

Woodall has been designing for dance, theatre and performance art groups since 1970. She has worked with numerous companies including the San Francisco Ballet, American Conservatory Theatre, the Joffrey Ballet, Dance Theater of Harlem, Smuin Ballet, the National Theater of Norway and the Hong Kong Ballet. She has received awards including DANCE/Bay Area Isadora Duncan Awards for Costume Design, Visual Design, and Sustained Achievement in Design. She also received the Bay Area Theatre Critics Circle Award for Costume Design.

Karen Young

Young designs costumes for dance, and also experimental theater and video art. She has designed for choreographers including Kyle Abraham, Brian Brooks and Lucinda Childs, and for companies including the Paul Taylor Dance Company, the Alvin Ailey American Dance Theater, American Ballet Theater and Miami City Ballet. She is the recipient of a design fellowship from the NEA and Theater Communications Group.

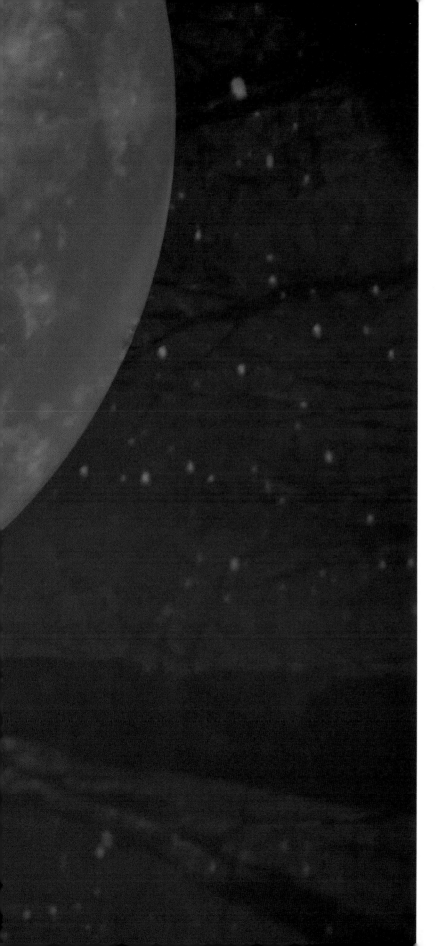

Introduction

Every time I watch [a dance] I see something different I hadn't seen before. And that's just thrilling. That's a living piece of art.

Holly Hynes, costume designer

Costumes are essential to create the mood of the piece . . . it's the first thing the audience sees. You are giving them the prologue of what they should be feeing or thinking or imagining this piece to be.

Nicole Haskins, choreographer

While all aspects of design play an important part in bringing a dance to life on stage, costume and dance have a special relationship. Both use the body as their medium of expression. The shapes the body creates as it moves and the relationships among the bodies on stage are products of the art made by both costume designers and choreographers. Whether the body is hidden in rippling waves of vivid silk or set off by a simple bandeau and shorts in the perfect neutral tone, choosing the right costume for a dance adds immeasurably to the work.

This is not a book about gussets. Or spandex. Or creating the perfect ombre dye treatment. There are resources already that teach the "how-tos" of costumes for dance. Rather, this book is a roadmap to collaboration for both choreographers and costume designers. It can be used as a text in both choreography and costume design courses, or as an enriching read for individuals looking to expand their own creativity. The emphasis is on contemporary and modern dance, but we touch on a wide range of styles. And, for those wanting a taste of the "how-tos" we have an Appendix with some tips for talking about and implementing dance costumes.

The Cowardly Lion played by Liang Fu in *The Wizard of Oz* at Kansas City Ballet (for more detail see Case Study #4)

The content of the book is largely derived from interviews with over 40 professional choreographers and costume designers whose experiences and anecdotes model a rich variety of collaboration methods. All of the quoted material comes from these interviews. A unique facet is that chapters on styles and methods are interspersed with "case studies." The author and the photographer visited dance companies to document costumes in performance. In-depth interviews with the choreographer and costume designer provide both vantage points on the evolution of each of the featured works. And photography by award-winning photographer Mitchell D. Wilson captures the vitality of the costumes and the dancers in motion, giving us the immediacy of live performance. None are posed or staged.

We sought to portray a range of styles of contemporary choreography and of costume, and to feature a diverse spectrum of artists in terms of personal identity, career path and geography. However, our aim was not to be a comprehensive survey of dance styles nor of current practitioners. Instead, a broad range of approaches to the creative process was the most essential type of diversity for this book.

I thought to write this book in order to continue my investigation into creative collaboration. After my first book, *Unbuttoned: The Art and Artists of Theatrical Costume Design*, I wanted to continue talking with artists about how they work, and the hugely variable process of designing for dance seemed a perfect fit. While I also design costumes professionally for theater and television, dance costume is often my favorite. The abstraction possible is very freeing, and the chance to be a part of a work as it takes shape is always thrilling. I began my professional design career in New York City designing for contemporary and modern dance. In my current job as a professor of costume design in a department of theatre and dance, I work on numerous pieces in ballet, jazz, tap and various styles of contemporary and modern dance choreographed by colleagues and guest artists. Collaborating with so many different choreographers has opened my eyes to the range of preferences for both dance costumes and their design process.

There is no right way to collaborate or to make art. As a teacher of design, I have found that learning how to explore freely is hard for novice artists. Costume designers are taught to be collaborators, and to be part of a team. However, the amount of flexibility needed to work in dance can be a learning curve for some and figuring out an approach to designing a work that does not yet fully exist can be daunting. The difficulty is not achieving a final product but learning how to productively develop ideas together—as a process rather than just a brainstorm. Constant evolution is more natural to choreographers—they learn improvisation as part of their training. For costume designers, the challenge is to find this same playfulness and ability to adapt.

Another goal of the book is to show choreographers the myriad ways that costumes can enhance the creative process, and how to communicate with and trust designers as members of the team. Often choreographers, particularly in modern and contemporary dance, do not have much chance to collaborate with costume designers. Dance studios and even university programs often have limited resources for designers and costume staff. Smaller professional companies are on tight budgets, and so they sometimes save by working with costume designers sparingly or not at all. Certain choreographers legitimately prefer to do their own costume design, and often other aspects of the process too, such as projections or lighting. But many others, because the experience has not been made available to them, are unaware of the richness that another collaborator can add to the mix.

With this book, I hope to help artists learn each other's language and evolve strategies to "translate" as they speak to each other.

A dancer in STATE choreographed by Ingri Fiksdal (for more detail, see Case Study #3)

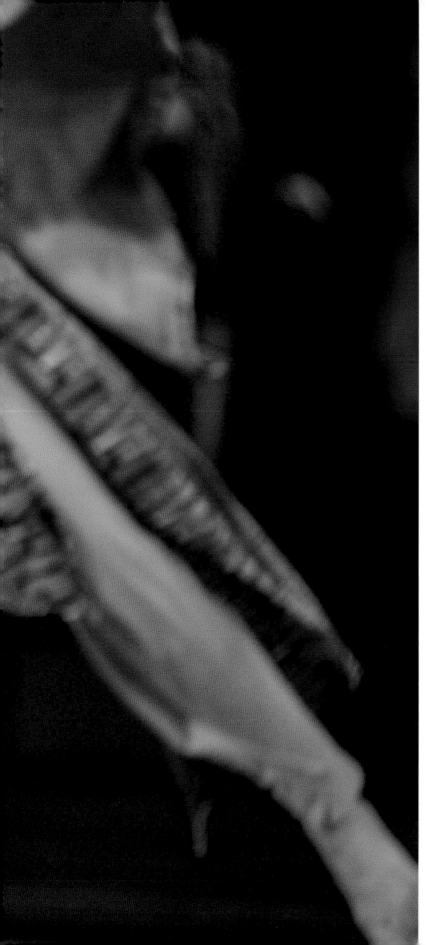

Case Study # 1

joyUS justUS

CHOREOGRAPHER—ANA MARIA ALVAREZ AND COMPANY

COMPANY—CONTRA-TIEMPO

PREMIERE DATE—NOVEMBER 2018

DATE PHOTOGRAPHED—NOVEMBER 2018

PERFORMANCE VENUE—CARPENTER PERFORMING ARTS CENTER IN LONG BEACH, CA

MUSIC—LAS CAFETERAS AND D. SABELA GRIMES

COSTUME DESIGN—CHARLESE ANTOINETTE

SCENIC DESIGN—EMILY ORLING

LIGHTING DESIGN—TUCE YASAK

Dancers Jasmine Stanley, Christopher Cuenza and Jannet Galdamez perform in *joyUS justUS*

Dancer Nathieli Diaz Bishop

A dancer crowned with flowers and wrapped in a striped shawl walks slowly but deliberately down the aisle of the theater and onto the stage. Almost like an invocation, she tilts her face up as she looks out at the audience and begins to recite a timeless message: We are all linked to the elements of the earth, we are all linked to each other. "You and I become Us." The mood shifts multiple times during the evening-length work. Joy takes multiple forms, from quiet reverence to exuberant energy, interrupted by words like *alien, illegal* and *slavery.* Dancers perform hip-hop duets and samba-influenced solos, and even gently pass one woman across a carpet of upturned feet. Musical accompaniment includes a retro-chic onstage band with traditional instruments rocking Afro-Mexican beats, a version of *This Land is Your Land* and a stunning array of vocalizations by one of the dancers. At the end of the night, the stage becomes a dance party, bringing the audience into the joyous catharsis.

"You and I become Us." This phrase is spoken repeatedly during the evening-length work *joyUS justUS,* in tones ranging from a murmur to a chorus. For Contra-Tiempo, a dance company that calls itself "Urban Latin Dance Theater," the practice of art must be rooted in community engagement and foster not only creativity but also social change. Founding Artistic Director Ana Maria Alvarez defines her choreography as "existing in the in-between . . . Salsa, Cuban, hip hop, contemporary—there's a place where all of those parts merge and there is this little space where they overlap, and that's were my work is located." In her merging of social and concert dance, Alvarez cites the influence of Katherine Dunham, who was a pioneer in bringing dance forms from the African diaspora to the concert dance stage.

In addition to its function for recreation, expression and human connection, social dance has traditionally also been used as a form of resistance. The act of dancing together can be an incredibly powerful bond and can uplift communities. "The premise [of the piece] is an exploration of joy as a radical act," Alvarez explained. Certain groups are often viewed from a perspective of deficit—words like under-served and under-privileged make it seem like the people they describe are lacking something fundamental. *JoyUS justUS* seeks to reframe the societal narrative. This work that she conceived and directed investigates "the idea that joy is one of those powerful weapons that we have, to build a world with more connection and more love. It's a reframing of justice: not thinking of justice as jailing people for breaking the law but the idea of justice being redemption and creating a world where people are being heard, loved and appreciated for their humanity."

While the company was still in the thick of performing their previous work, *Agua Furiosa,* the dancers were surprised to learn that Alvarez had already begun thinking about their next project. The work, loosely based on Shakespeare's *the Tempest,* was emotionally draining to perform, and inspired her to develop a new work in reaction. "It had a message of hope right at the end, but we all needed soul showers after every performance," Alvarez explained. "It wasn't an accident that the following work was . . . an incredible cathartic work about joy."

The content of *joyUS justUS* came from narratives gathered not only from the diverse company of dancers who perform in the piece, but also from the people of South Los Angeles. For Alvarez "us" is the collective us, *nosotros* in Spanish. Contra-Tiempo did community outreach jam and discussion "*sabor* sessions" (Spanish for *flavor*) in many neighborhoods for other works. For *joyUS justUS* they did weekly sessions on the practice of "radical joy" for two years, in just one community in South LA. They built strong connections with the residents, many of whom attended multiple times. "Also, joy is very triggering for people," explains Alvarez. "We create together, move together, relate together. And we work together. We move our bodies and feel great." As the piece began to take shape, Alvarez and the dancers showed sections of it and got feedback. They then asked the community to try some of the movement and then adapt it into their own version. After the showing of choreography, they would spend time "in council," a story circle rooted in many indigenous peoples' practices around the world, discussing reactions and responses. As the group shared more stories, Alvarez noticed certain themes repeating. Even as she adjusted the prompts, mothers and mothering kept coming up. "We realized how much this piece [and joy itself] is connected to our relationship to mother, [and] to mother earth. Not just like a mother and child but mothering like nurturing, creating a space for people to grow and be their best selves."

The first year of development consisted of Alvarez doing her own research and thinking, and the community outreach sessions. In addition to the source material from collaborators, she referred to three major texts. The Dalai Lama's conversation about joy with South African Bishop Desmond Tutu, *The Book of Joy,* was a seminal influence. She learned about embracing chaos and change from *Emergent Strategy: Shaping Change, Changing Worlds* by adrienne maree brown. *Emergent Strategy* showed her how the use of collectives, rather than a hierarchy, was essential to create art and change. To help combine the dual influences of mother and mother earth,

(Above and below) dancer Samad Raheem

Cuenza and Raheem with the band Las Cafeteras seen behind

she read *Braiding Sweetgrass* by Robin Wall Kimmerer, an activist ecologist, about the link between our relationship with nature and how we connect with society. The four elements (earth, air, wind and fire) became one of the themes that she worked into the piece. While exploring these ideas, Alvarez realized that to truly apply them, she had to use them more broadly than just in the choreography. "As we were starting to do this work, our own organization had to figure out what does it mean to be a social justice dance company. Inside of this idea of the collective us and emergence, is there still hierarchy? There is still dancer crediting. [We were] building a dance company inside of a capitalist notion of how to survive as an artist."

The second year of the development moved into generating the actual material for the piece, both choreography and text. Alvarez created movement phrases that the dancers collectively developed into larger sections. The dancers also generated choreography, and one dancer in particular, Samad Guerra, was a major contributor to the script as well. "He was writing a lot of text about the justice system and around his experience growing up in the Bay Area as a black man," Alvarez recounts. "What did that look like and what did that mean inside all of the things we are talking about?" During the dance, the performers sometimes speak text on stage, and at other times the story is prerecorded, ranging from Alvarez telling about meeting her adopted son for the first time to layered sounds of protests and gunshots.

Another major collaborator was the band Las Cafeteras, whose style is influenced by a range of roots music from Afro-Mexican to Americana, mixing electronic and acoustic along with four vocalists. While Contra-Tiempo had done small collaborations with them before, this was the first time the two groups performed a whole production together. "We always joke that they are the music version of Contra-Tiempo and Contra-Tiempo is the dance version of Las Cafeteras. We are so incredibly aligned in terms of our politics and our approach to narrative and to creating a world of more love and justice and connection," Alvarez said. The debut performance of *joyUS justUS* in Los Angeles included the band live on stage, although the dancers will have to tour with a recording of the music.

Once the piece was in the second year of development, Alvarez was ready to bring in a costume designer to begin collaboration. "Costumes were part of my initial vision—everyone would be an individual, in bright colors, reflective of who they were as people. But also delving into who they were culturally and who they felt connected to. And *where* they felt connected to." Alvarez had not worked with Charlese Antoinette before, but after meeting her at the suggestion of some of the dancers, decided she was the right designer for this project. "A lot of the time dance costume is just about creating clean lines for the dancer's body, but this was about the costumes being another character in the story. I didn't want regular clothes, but clothes that are like a full, accentuated version of ourselves. They are pretty wild, complicated, even chaotic. Not linear but spirals . . . a tangled web of humanity."

Antoinette designs for a variety of media, ranging from styling commercials to shows like *Raising Don* for Netflix, as well as stage work. She was eager to work with Contra-Tiempo because of the way the group bridges communities. "I don't think there are many artists that are having this conversation in this way. It's deeply personal to everyone in the company and to Ana Maria [Alvarez]. Being in LA there is a huge divide [between black and brown]."

Antoinette joined the process not long before a showing at Lincoln Center, about 11 months before the premiere, and she had to work rapidly. She met with Alvarez about the overall ideas for the piece. They talked about concepts, and Alvarez showed some images to give a general flavor. The choreographer had some definite ideas about which dancers should be in certain shapes—like pants or a full skirt—to complement the kinds of movement they were doing, but otherwise she left the specifics to the designer. Since the piece was based so closely on the group's varied identities, Antoinette interviewed the dancers as her next step. The designer talked to them about who they were as people and about their ethnic and cultural backgrounds, as well as about their personal style. "The show is very much about community, about not being ashamed to be who you are. With all the political turmoil going on right now, [it's about] finding joy as people of color, although things going on can steal your joy. It's a very powerful message and I wanted to be sure that each person felt empowered in their costume," Antoinette explained. After the interviews, she "digested it all" and then put together some mood boards of research and met with the choreographer again. While her next step would usually be to do sketches, there wasn't time before the showing, and so she jumped right to putting looks together on the dancers during fittings, using preexisting clothing in a collage-like process. After getting dancer and choreographer approval for the direction she was heading, she had some pieces custom-made to get the shapes, colors and patterns that she wanted.

Research into the cultural backgrounds of the dancers inspired some of her costume designs. She noted the overlap in ancestry,

Members of the company lift Jasmine Stanley with their feet

Galdamez performs a solo with members of Las Cafeteras

Galdamez and Raheem

Iris Avalos and Biana Medina lead an emotional moment

especially in the Caribbean diaspora, between Spanish-speaking people and those of African ancestry. This is one of the reasons she used African fabrics on many of the performers. She looked at the Sapeurs in the Congo as inspiration for the costume for Samad Guerra. The Sapeurs wear brightly colored suits and have dance battles. "I wanted him to feel formal. He is kind of like the narrator, he weaves the story together, so it was important that he stood out in a way and also that there was a nod to his African ancestry." Another dancer, Isis Avalos, is Mexican American, and both she and Antoinette are fans of Frida Kahlo, so the designer wanted to include a nod to the painter. She used a flower crown and a cape woven with a distinct ethnic pattern that Avalos wears in some of the piece, although she takes it off for some of the more active

sections. "Chris [Cuenza] is Filipino and his costume also nodded towards the skirts that Filipino men wear. His favorite is hip hop and he does a lot of movement with his legs," Antoinette said. She designed a fringe-like skirt for him out of leather. Alvarez liked the idea and commented that his look also supported her desire to reference Maori warriors, who "look like they are really fighting for something powerful."

Antoinette used her color choices to tie the costumes to the four elements, one of the thematic aspects of the dance. Diana Toledo was one of the dancers who represented fire, and Antoinette loved how her blue hair complemented her mostly red costume and felt like part of the flame. To communicate joy, she used bright colors and a lot of shine and sparkle. "I tried to design costumes that

Stanley and Avalos cry out

brought across this idea of joy in being who you are." Antoinette described her goal for the work as creating "things that were real, that you could see in a magazine or street style, but elevated." She made the clothing work for dance by using stretch fabrics, and also by ensuring that the costumes would create their own movement. By doing things like adding slits into the sides of pants, she "tried to make everything dynamic and move with them, so nothing was static . . . I love fringe. By the time we got done I realized I had put fringe on a lot of people. It's great for movement."

After the showing in New York, Antoinette had a chance to edit her designs. She adapted some of the designs, and had some additional pieces built. Some costumes got additional decoration and others were changed more fundamentally. Jannet Galdamez represents

the Trinidadian goddess of water, and she needed a full skirt. She manipulates it with her hands, swirling it as she moves. Choreographer and designer decided that the original version was not big enough, and so Antoinette made the ruffled blue and yellow skirt larger and more dramatic. Antoinette decided that the track pants she had for Shantel Ureña, while capturing her "tomboy" flavor, were too pedestrian and her costume didn't fit in aesthetically with the rest. She added trim to her shirt, and had purple sparkly pants made that felt more tailored to the dancer's body but were still fun and dynamic.

While this design process was not her typical way of working, Antoinette enjoyed the experiment. "This way, we got to play. I got to take things that were simple and not exciting and add a lot of

Medina strikes a pose

Avalos with her Frida Kahlo-inspired flower crown

Diana Toledo

crazy stuff to it." Antoinette also appreciated the chance to let her personal aesthetic be more prominent in the design. The majority of her work is in more commercial projects where this is not an option. She also enjoyed having "fewer cooks in the kitchen," as compared with her work in film and television. She only had to clear ideas with Alvarez and the dancers, as opposed to directors, producers and a whole battery of people who weigh in on the details during screen work.

Alvarez was very happy with the costumes and thought they had a "very reciprocal relationship with the work." They inspired her to commission artist and designer Emily Orling to design "altar quilts" to serve as a backdrop for the piece. While her first thought for a background was projections, she decided that something more tangible would be more fitting. "Quilts make me think about women creating beauty out of scraps. You can see the collage of colors and patterns, creating identity." When the dancers met "in council" with community members, they used an altar with a cloth in the center of the circle. Orling incorporated that cloth into the quilts, as well as vibrant colors and patterns inspired by the costumes. Alvarez noted that "In many ways we are taking the incredible energy and vibration that the people in South LA shared with us and it's [literally] in the piece with us." The idea of a community altar also followed from the workshops to the finished piece. As part of every performance, some audience members are seated onstage, as part of the work, and there is a set-up of candles flanking them at the sides of the stage.

The costumes also inspired Alvarez to add an audience participation facet. The company laid scarf-sized scraps of fabric over each seat in the auditorium before the show, and the audience was encouraged to wave them during the event like a rally towel at a sporting event. Since the audience tended to take them home, they had to switch from using scraps from the actual costumes to substituting other fabric with the same general appearance.

During the piece the dancers perform solos, each in their own personal style and at other times they dance as a group. The costumes echo this. They give an overall aesthetic to the group, but each dancer stands out as an individual visually as well as choreographically. The sections of the piece vary from soft and introspective to bold and vibrant, and the text varies from topical references to hoodies and skittles to more universal stories of mothers and children. Boundaries blur. Dancers also play percussion; band members join the formations downstage. In one section, the dancers move in a more standard "contemporary dance" style, pacing at right angles around the boundaries of a cage-like grid of harsh white projections on the floor. The music gradually changes to just percussion, and one dancer does a phrase based on traditional Afro-Cuban dance. As the phrase repeats, the rest of the company breaks out of the grid one at a time and joins her. They do the phrase together, creating a stirring show of unity.

The ensemble and Las Cafeteras in front of Emily Orling's altar quilts

1

Role of Design and Costumes in and for Dance

This chapter provides background information crucial to the understanding of costume for dance. Some readers may be familiar with this content and skim over these sections or use them merely for reference.

HISTORICAL OVERVIEW

As far as historians can determine, the practice of dance is nearly as old as humanity. People have always moved their bodies expressively to tell stories, worship gods, to pass the time and to impress others. The urge to embellish the dancer followed soon after the practice began. Masks, face paint and costumes became the earliest type of visual design used in performance. Costume, and especially masks, transformed the wearer into someone else. For some cultures, the transformation was merely suggested, for others it was believed to be actual, and a mask or covering took away the dancer's own identity and made them into a conduit for the spirits.[1]

Early dance performances used costumes adapted from day-to-day clothing, but also tasked artists with imagining and producing entirely novel structures, materials and surface decoration that would surprise and delight the viewer. The environment of a dance also became important for some cultures. Whether they created backdrops, raised platforms, carried banners or used existing locations that gave the desired ambiance, the setting as a part of the overall effect became a factor. Early cultures had only limited

Devin Baker, Matthew J. Talley, Robert Pulido, Quentin ApolloVaughn Sledge and Michael Green of Dayton Contemporary Dance Company perform *Promontory* by Kevin Ward, costume design by Kevin Ward

A detail of a costume designed by Charlese Antoinette from *joyUS justUS* by Contra-Tiempo dance company

lighting options, but the choice to perform by sunlight, moonlight, campfire or torch conveyed mood. Darker performance settings added mystery and atmosphere. Sound in the form of music, percussion and vocalizations originated as early as dance, and music and sound effects were a vital part of the earliest dances.

Many cultures evolved a tradition of formal dance performances. Most originated in religious ritual, but also strove to capture the audience's imagination and attention. Tribes of the northern plains in America performed dances to mark events, welcome visitors, for spiritual rituals and for entertainment. One that has survived to the present day is the grass dance, although it has evolved and adapted.[2] Accounts of the exact origins of the dance differ, but it incorporates the portrayal

of swaying movements of the grasses, and the costume follows suit. Originally the dancers tied braided grass into their belts; later versions featured long strands of fibers and fringe that create a fancier version of the same effect.[3] Ancient Greek festivals featured performances that combined dance and music in the *dithyramb*. And dances were performed as separate sections within tragedies and comedies.[4] Large audiences assembled for religious festivals in specially built arenas. The performers wore exaggerated facial expressions in the form of masks and used movement and rhythm to project the grand tales to the very back row. The costumes and masks helped audiences to identify the characters. Many Asian cultures also evolved dramatic dance-based entertainment. Hindus in India had professional dancers

Dancers of Time Lapse Dance performing *Wind Rose* by Jody Sperling, costume design by Mary Jo Mecca (for more detail see Case Study #5)

Lauren Terry and Aubrey Hyde of Nashville Ballet perform *The Four Seasons* choreographed by Paul Vasterling, costume design by David Heuvel

termed *devadasis*, who served in temples and performed in royal courts.[5] They used dance, gesture, music and poetry to tell stories in a style that is now termed classical dance of India, one of the oldest forms of which is Bharatanatyam. The costumes accentuated the dance and made the bejeweled performers mesmerizing to watch. In the seventeenth century, the Japanese began to perform Kabuki, merging song, dance and acrobatics with the performance of stories. They used ingenious scenery to enable special effects and wore elaborate wigs and makeup. Costume changes happened onstage, as part of the overall spectacle of the event.[6]

In European performances, costumes and scenery also became an expected component for both theater and dance, and the two forms merged in operas and masques. When realistic painted scenery came into use in Europe during the Renaissance, artists were sought to design the elaborate perspective effects. Costumes, scenery and eventually lighting conveyed elements of a ballet's story and setting to audiences. Beyond storytelling, the visuals also impressed them with beauty and theatrical effects. The iconic mid-nineteenth-century Romantic-era ballet *La Sylphide* portrayed the ballerinas as spirits, their ethereal nature enhanced by dancing en pointe in gauzy costumes illuminated with flickering gas lighting.[7]

By the twentieth century, concert dance diverged into multiple forms that used design in varying ways. Ballet, especially story ballets, continued traditions of decorative costumes and scenery. Jazz and tap, particularly when performed in vaudeville and revues, also used elaborate design elements. Some modern dance companies used conventional scenery to portray a story or an exotic location while others included abstract backdrops or set pieces to accentuate themes. However, much of modern dance sought to pare down the stage picture to its essentials, a practice that endures today in many styles of contemporary dance. Although with rare exceptions costumes were not eliminated entirely, they were often very simple, and many works did not use scenery at all. Some used minimal music, perhaps just percussion, or performed in silence. Lighting technology steadily progressed over the century, however, and the importance of lighting design grew. A sense of environment and texture on the bare stage could be created with colors and patterns of light, and the three-dimensional space could be defined with light and shadow.

In the later twentieth century and into the twenty-first, design has become an increasingly important element across dance styles. Some artists do still prefer to keep the emphasis on the choreography and use design in a de-emphasized supporting role. However, others embrace additional elements, and use varying combinations of scenery, projections, elaborate costumes or perhaps even puppetry.

The importance of costume, scenery, lighting and sound as elements of dance performance has ebbed and flowed over time. And the role of the designer itself has evolved. Earlier traditions in both theater and dance did not consider design a noteworthy job. In European traditions, composers wrote music, and sometimes artists designed backdrops, but the overall visual style of a production was not usually thought of as something to be developed by a team of expert artists until the later nineteenth century. Lighting, even after technology allowed more than just dimming and brightening, was initially considered mainly a technical field. The artistry of lighting a space was only gradually acknowledged. A few known artists designed costumes as far back as the renaissance, but for most of that era through the beginning of the twentieth century, the garments worn by performers were decided upon by directors, choreographers or the performers themselves. Anonymous tailors and seamstresses created costumes that followed fashion and stage traditions. The job of costume designer, a professional who considered the look of the individual costumes in conjunction with the overall concept of the dance, was slow to evolve. One notable exception to this was the Ballets Russes, which sought unity for each ballet, not just choreographically but also in the visuals.[8] Under the direction of producer Sergei Diaghilev, scenery and costumes were commissioned from some of the most famous artists of the time, including Pablo Picasso and Henri Matisse.

In current practice, stage designers not only produce beautiful gowns or perfectly timed blackouts, they also participate in the overall creation of a production. Designers execute the vision of the choreographer, but they also help to define what that vision is, and how best to translate the ideas into scenery, costume, light or sound.

IMPORTANCE OF DESIGN FOR DANCE

Design is the process of making choices.

During interviews for this book, when selecting which of their works to discuss, choreographers often stated that a given work didn't truly have costume design because the costumes were not custom-made. Or that a very simple costume was not really a costume design. How a costume design is implemented does not make it more or less of a design. A dress can be custom-made, but as an exact copy of a dress from a vintage fashion photo. And very creative ideas can be realized through shopping or pulling from stock. The difference is comparable to the one between the art of painting, where the image is created completely, and the arts of photography or collage, where the image is selected or assembled from preexisting or found elements. The amount of time spent also does not make something a more or less valid design. A piece of jersey quickly wrapped around the body can be just as fabulous as an intricate dress made of 18 separate pieces out of three types of silk. It might take more time to ponder options and finally select a pale gray tank and shorts than to decide on a set of unitards each hand-painted with markings from a different species of butterfly.

Function of Stage Design

The various design fields including costume, lighting, scenery, sound and sometimes also properties, puppets or video/digital projection, can deepen and enrich a dance. Individually and collectively, the areas of design help the work to communicate with an audience. If the work has a narrative, the visuals and sounds can convey information about the overall setting or environment of the piece and who its inhabitants are. If a work is more abstract, the design performs the same function, albeit in a less evident and literal way. In many cases, just as the flying leaps of a dancer should feel as natural as walking, designers have been successful if their work is not explicitly noticed by the audience.

Design can use imagery, music and sound to bring out themes in a work. It also can evoke moods or help to create a point of view. The different areas might all work in similar ways to communicate. Or they might convey different aspects of a work, or purposely contrast and even clash with each other. The design might create a warm, rich, subtle feeling with costumes in earth-toned velvets, a soft-edged pool of amber light that pulls the viewer towards center stage, deep slow cello music enhanced by reverberation in the sound system and hanging scenic pieces of over-scale tapestry, the woven threads each as wide as a rope. Or, a work might show the alienation of city dwellers by putting dancers impeccably dressed in modern business suits in front of scrolling projections of fish in an aquarium, dancing to hard-edged grunge music that alternately emanates from speakers on the left and right sides of the auditorium.

Overall, the evolution of ideas between collaborators can be one of the most satisfying parts of the creative process. For some artists, the journey is actually the most important aspect of their art. Choreographer Trey McIntyre thinks of dance as a puzzle to solve: "I am way more interested in the process than the product. I think it's great to have a goal of a performance in the end because it makes the process happen, but the more exploratory the better. The more a designer wants to go down the path with me, the better."

Function of Costume Design

Costume, defined as clothing worn for performance, affects the dancer's body, the movements in the dance, and the overall dance itself. It also affects the viewer's perception of these three elements. A well-planned costume takes all of these aspects into consideration.

The difference between costume and fashion is not the product but the intent. If someone happens to be wearing a leotard, a velvet ball-gown or a graphic T-shirt and corduroys to rehearsal and performs a dance, it is fashion. If that outfit was specifically chosen to accompany that dance, then it is a costume. Especially when referring to historical styles, the terms *fashion* and *costume* are sometimes used interchangeably, which can be confusing. For those trained in fashion schools, the word costume can have a negative connotation, meaning something overdone, too flamboyant or "costumey."

Through corsetry or padding, a costume can actually alter the shape of the body. Or, more commonly, the costume can just give the impression of a different body shape. The change can be subtle, like a sleeveless floor length jumpsuit that creates a strong vertical column from shoulder to heel and thus appears to lengthen the body. Or a garment can create stronger illusions like hiding curves to make an adult woman seem like a child. Clothing can emphasize, pull focus from, reveal or hide different parts of the body. Placement of seams and textures of fabrics can flatter the shape and line of the body. Beyond the basic form of the body, costume can also bring out characteristics specific to the performer. Those can be physical, like showcasing muscularity or contrasting a dark costume with translucent pale skin. Or, the costume can transmit the personality of a dancer—perhaps a quirky color combination seems to sum them up, or their tendency to hide in infinity scarves could inspire loops of fabric wound around the body.

Costume can affect the actual movement of the performer. The fit and materials can either restrict movement or enable complete freedom. A stiff platter tutu allows only certain types of floor work. Long flowing fringe that keeps moving forward when the dancer stops suddenly affects the way they end a turn. Beyond logistics, the costume can also subtly affect the movement quality as it partners with the dancer. Trailing sleeves might add nuance to arm movements and dodging them adds extra responsiveness during partnering. The costume can also change the way movement feels to a dancer. The support of a structured vest might give a sense of verticality. Or a skirt of ostrich plumes transforms an ordinary walk into the strut of a bird.

The costume also adds to the meaning and experience of the overall dance. A deep purple dress accented with only a narrow gold belt shows the austerity of the vanquished queen. A costume decked with sudsy ruffles of pink and aqua evokes springtime. Whether a costume helps a dancer portray a character in a story, or whether the addition of a knit hat in an abstract piece enhances the dancer's essential humanity, the costume in this case relates to the dancer's performance, rather than the performer themselves. And, of course whether in a narrative or abstract work, costume can show connections, make groupings or underline differences between dancers. Red edging on a blouse can highlight the featured dancer in a group of peasant girls. Use of sheer and opaque fabrics might show the difference between fairy and human characters. Or, over the four movements of a piece, the costumes of the entire group could progress from pale aqua to deep navy other than one dancer who remains in aqua, gradually standing out more and more from the rest of the cast.

FIELDS OF STAGE DESIGN

This book examines the particulars of collaboration between costume designers and choreographers, but that collaboration should not exist in a vacuum. Ideally, all the components of a production would be known at the outset of a project—what kind of music will it have? What kind of space will it perform in? Will there be scenery? Whether the choreographer meets with the whole team as a group at the outset or whether conversations happen in sequence, the artists involved need to know how their work will fit into the whole. If the lighting designer will not join a project until just before dress rehearsals, a choreographer should let the costume designer know that she plans to use lots of silhouette or that the piece will begin in very dim light, gradually brightening to visibility. This would have a major impact on planning shapes or colors of costumes.

Choreographer Paul Vasterling notes the importance of all the different design areas, but that each speak their own language. In initial meetings about concepts with designers, he "tells each the same story. They listen to it differently." Conversations with costume designers tend to be much longer-term. He finds that there is more back and forth because costume deals with "the direct instrument that is expressing what we want to express. The costume and the dancer are one thing—it's very obvious, but they become a unit and you have to know what you are dealing with. The lighting is a bit more like costuming [in its effect on the dancer] and the scenery is the frame."

Sound and Music

Music is one of the fields most intrinsically linked with dance. Most typically, music exists first, and then dance steps are created to follow it. Some choreographers choose preexisting music, while others collaborate with a composer. Some wait until a work is mostly complete before adding a score, and others don't use music at all, instead dancing in silence or to poetry. Sound design is linked to music but is not the same thing, and in most cases sound designer and composer are two separate jobs. A sound designer chooses specific sounds that will be used, and also the way in which they will be delivered. If music is performed live, they adjust the balance and sound quality the audience hears, whether amplified or acoustic. They also work with live sound on stage, such as microphones for tap sounds or speaking. Sound designers use recorded sound and do alterations ranging from subtly enhancing a recording to creating an entire soundscape of layered noises and snippets of dialog.

Lighting

In current-day concert dance, lighting is often the most prevalent aspect of design. While dancers can wear their own jeans or leotards and dance on a bare stage, they cannot light themselves. Like dance, lighting exists not only in space but in time. It can change gradually or suddenly over the course of the piece and moves as fluidly as the dancers. The lighting designer chooses the direction the light will come from, the colors that will be used, and the way the lighting instruments will combine over the duration of the piece. Through angle, intensity and color, lighting creates mood and controls what the audience does and does not see. Lighting can also create an environment for a dance. Whether by use of patterns of shadow on the floor or by creating a sunset-like gradient from yellow to red behind the dancers, lighting can enhance scenery or be the scenery.

Scenery

Scenery is much less associated with contemporary dance than other design elements. However, it plays an important role in many works. Scenery can be a decorative surround for the dancers or it can be something that they climb on or even dance with. Backdrops can portray a location, whether colorful painted trees overlap to form a fantastical forest or a chain-link fence and basketball net define an urban playground. Scenic elements might not strive to create an environment at all, but rather be visual art to accent or comment on the dance. Oversized portraits of faces, collages of abstract color, sculptural mounds of plastic bottles or scrawled graffiti can all add to a dance. Whether dancers lay across chairs or climb on a scaffold of steel pipes, scenery can become an active part of the choreography. Fabric panels hanging from the ceiling can break up the space, as dancers pass in front of and behind them, or become streamers that the dancers pull into diagonals and curves.

Projections and Digital Media

Projection is related to scenery but is considered its own area of design in most cases. Whether video or stills, projection designers select images or create their own, and then edit them into sequences timed to the dance. Projections are most typically used like scenery, putting images on a screen or surface behind the choreography. However, they can also be projected onto the dancers themselves, blurring the live and the filmed. In most cases, images are prerecorded. However, some works use live video, enabling the audience to see a mirrored performance: live bodies dancing alongside oversized two-dimensional images of themselves.

Properties (Props)

Properties are another sub-category of scenery but can also be considered a separate area of design. There is no exact line where objects become too small to be scenery and instead count as props, but usually furniture is part of scenery, even relatively small pieces like chairs. Props can be objects that establish character or narrative, like a teddy bear or newspaper. An object might be an active part of the dance: the performer carries a bowl to center stage, kneels in front of it, and then dips out handfuls of rice that he pours in spirals onto the floor. Dancing with props is a common convention in many styles of dance, whether fans, canes or scarves. Fred Astaire even famously used a coat rack as a dance partner.

Makeup

Makeup is often considered a sub-field of costume, as are hair and wigs. However, it can also be its own field with its own expertise required. Traditional dance forms of many cultures use makeup, often in ways that completely transform the human face. But beyond simple conveyance of beauty and enhancing features, makeup is not a common aspect of contemporary Western dance. However, many do incorporate it, in ways that range from painting stylized feathers as part of a bird costume to character effects like exaggerated features for a witch in a fairytale. Makeup can be also used in less expected ways, like dancers gradually smearing their bright red lipstick across their cheeks over the course of a dance. While most typically used on the face, makeup can be applied to the body as well.

DESIGN AS COMMUNICATION

The task of creating a design is in the choosing. When designing a custom-made dress, a nearly endless spectrum of options are available: the length of the skirt, the shape of the sleeve, the placement of the waistline, the weight and drape of the fabric. However, even if the choice is just between one of the three colors of leggings that the company owns a set of, a design decision has still been made, and black leggings will give a piece a very different character than red when worn with dark gray tops. And whether the choices are made by a designer or a choreographer, the set of decisions they make still add up to a design.

For purposes of collaboration and communication, it can be helpful to define basic design terms. However, all artists use and interpret parameters differently, so verbal discussions should be supplemented by examples of images or movement to be sure everyone is on the same page.

Color is one of the most basic variables in design, and one of the most important. Color evokes strong associations and emotions, both personal and cultural. Many designers and choreographers see color as they listen to music, or feel certain hues based on how the dancers move. When considering a color, three basic aspects come into play. *Hue* is the basic color itself—red, green, purple. Hues can be varied by *value*, which is how pale or dark they are. A tint of red is pale pink, and a shade of red is a dark wine tone. The last variable is *saturation*, which is how intense the color is. Highly saturated lime green dials down to browner or grayer tones like olive. For costume, color comes from fabric and is created with pigment. While a topic too expansive for this book, discussions of color should differentiate between color of pigment and color of light. Colors of light mix and vary in an entirely different fashion. For stage work, scenery and costume must ensure their colors are compatible with colors of light being used.

Costume and dance are both visual mediums made up of forms in space. A costume has its own form, and when worn it also becomes a part of the dancer's form. An arrangement of forms or masses in a space (or on a body, in the case of a single costume) makes a *composition*. The building block of form is line. In art and design, a *line* is something with one dimension, a path from one point to another. A line can have different visual qualities. It can be straight or curved, and its path can give different energies and movement qualities: an irregular zigzag as compared with a gradual arc. The expansion into two dimensions, a flat shape, is often called a *silhouette* when referring to costumes. The three-dimensional version of a shape is referred to in art and design as *mass* or *volume*. The shape of a costume might be organic or geometric, symmetrical or jagged, full or narrow.

The term *line* is very important for dance. In many styles of dance, the word refers not only to the angles of the limbs, but also to the direction and shape of the entire body as it extends in space. Good lines for a dancer are not just about seeming long or outstretched, but about subtle nuances of angle and shape that enhance the overall aesthetic. The line of the dancer's body affects the shape the costume makes during a dance. A costume also has its own lines, separate from the movement of the dancer. A vest might have strong diagonals, whether from a diagonally striped fabric or from a bottom edge that makes a sharp V-shape front and back. A unitard might be painted with spirals that wind up the body like a corkscrew, giving movement even when the dancer is still. The edges of a costume are often a consideration of line and shape for both garment and wearer. Leggings create a different proportion when they end just below the calf muscle than when they stop at the ankle. Softly draped necklines hide and reveal collarbones and shoulder blades, whereas strong V-shapes cut across them.

Texture and pattern are another important consideration. *Texture* can be actual, like velvet, or implied, like a softness from varying colors of threads in a space-dye technique. *Pattern* gives a surface decoration to the body, which—depending on how it is used—can help to define its edges or obscure them. Clearly fabrics are the most important textural element in costume. How they look and move on the body stems from their consistency and weight. Satins slide across the body, while crisp linens crumple.

PRODUCTION PROCESS FOR DANCE

For those unfamiliar with working in dance, it can be helpful to understand the different steps of the process from start to finish. This is a general overview, and different artists and companies might use different orders, or skip some of these steps.

Conceptualization and Planning

Any piece must start with initial conversations between collaborators. The timing may vary. Sometimes everyone starts together with the choreographer, other times music may start first, then costume, and lighting much later. Some choreographers develop the work for quite a while alone, and then work with collaborators once they have ideas mostly worked out. Others bring in everyone right at the beginning for brainstorming sessions.

Rehearsal Period

Quite logically, once the choreographer is rehearsing with dancers, they are in the rehearsal period. Length of rehearsal time varies from a few weeks to months to years. Depending on the time needed to implement the costume design, ideas might be developed during the rehearsal process, or they might have to be finished prior, so the costumes can be built, fit and tested ahead of the performance.

Showings

Some choreographers do showings, which are informal performances of work in progress to get feedback from audiences or fellow artists, or to get backing from producers. These might happen without costumes at all, just in rehearsal clothes, or they can be a chance to test out costume ideas. Showings are more likely to be done in a studio-type space than on a stage, so the other design elements like lighting might also be simplified or left out.

Blocking or Spacing Rehearsals

Once the work is about to head into the performance venue, dancers get a chance to work out movement and spacing on the stage. These rehearsals are usually done without any design elements other than those that take up space, such as large skirts or pieces of scenery.

Technical Rehearsals

Technical rehearsals happen in the performance space, and their purpose is to introduce the design elements into the work, in sync with the choreography and with each other. Technical rehearsals are not for polishing choreography and movement. Instead, the goal is to evaluate the design, and ensure it is working in context with the dance. If there is live music, it is usually not used at this point. The rehearsal typically follows a stop and go timeline, rather than running the work straight through, and dancers often mark the movement instead of dancing it full out. The emphasis tends to be on lighting, since there is no good way to test lighting ideas prior to being in the theater. Any other elements that involve

Dancers LaMoi Leon Hedrington and Dorsey Brown from Dayton Contemporary Dance Company perform Urban Milonga by Alvin Rangel, costume design by L'Amour Ameer.

cueing and timing or are affected by the physical space of the performance venue are also a focus of technical rehearsals: scene changes, lighting cues, sound levels, possibly costume changes. During technical rehearsals the designers, choreographer and stage manager check that the various elements work together as planned and make adjustments as needed. The designers ensure that projections balance with lighting so both dancers and video are visible. The run crew practices a set change until it happens within eight bars of the music. The stage manager paces the falling snow so that it evokes a gentle flurry and doesn't cover the stage until the final duet. Sometimes these rehearsals happen in costume, sometimes not. However, technical rehearsals can be a time to test out a costume in the space, under lights. A dancer may

need to be sure they can climb stairs or fit through a door in their full-skirted tutu. The costume designer might want to see that the angle of the light shows a glittering fabric to advantage. The lighting designer might want to check that the choreographer and costume designer like the way the red jacket looks as the lights shift from amber to blue.

Dress Rehearsal

A dress rehearsal is a run-through of the work with minimal stops if any, mimicking an actual performance without an audience. Full costumes, scenery, props, lighting, music and any other technical elements and the dancing are done at performance quality. Some companies also have previews, which use a live audience although the work is still being edited and adjusted.

By opening night, everything is finished.

NOTES

1 Barbara S. Glass, *African American Dance: An Illustrated History* (Jefferson: McFarland & Company, 2012), 7.

2 Margaret Fuhrer, *American Dance: The Complete Illustrated History* (Minneapolis: Voyageur Press, 2014), 19.

3 "Grass Dance," Native Spirit, accessed May 28, 2020, www.nativespirit.com/grass-dance.php

4 Jack Anderson, *Ballet & Modern Dance: A Concise History* (Hightstown: Princeton Book Company, 1992), 17.

5 Patricia Leigh Beaman, *World Dance Cultures: From Ritual to Spectacle* (New York: Routledge, 2018), section 1.2.

6 Beaman, *World Dance Cultures*, section 4.3.

7 Anderson, *Ballet & Modern Dance*, 78.

8 Anderson, *Ballet & Modern Dance*, 123.

Case Study #2

In My Your Head

CHOREOGRAPHER—JOY BOLLINGER

COMPANY—BRUCE WOOD DANCE

PREMIERE DATE—NOVEMBER 2019

DATE PHOTOGRAPHED—NOVEMBER 2019

PERFORMANCE VENUE—MOODY PERFORMANCE HALL IN DALLAS, TX

MUSIC—RADIOHEAD

COSTUME DESIGN—JOHN AHRENS

LIGHTING DESIGN—TONY TUCCI

The final moment of In My Your Head, when the dancers tap on the scrim upstage

A line of dancers emerges from the wings, making mechanized gestures with their hands. They move forward gradually, side by side, enclosed by a rectangle of harsh white light that moves with them, pulling them like a tractor beam towards the center stage. Suddenly the music shifts into high gear, and the dancers and the lighting explode out in all directions, shattering the formation.

"I'm not trying to make a statement. I am talking about something that affects me and letting that make the statement." Joy Bollinger, the Artistic Director of Bruce Wood Dance, found the current political climate moved her to create a more contemporary piece. She pulled away from her usual balletic style set to classical music. Instead, the music of Radiohead fit her mindset. "The idea for the work was looking at the effects of an ever-fragile and uncertain political and emotional landscape. The piece itself travels through frustration, anger and disillusionment back to a sense of feeling lost or confused. And then it ends somber but hopeful."

Bollinger spent 12 years as a dancer with Bruce Wood Dance, performing in more than 50 of his works, and she learned from Wood's humanistic approach to modern ballet. Since Wood's untimely death in 2014, she became Rehearsal Director and then Artistic Director. Although *In My Your Head* is only her third choreographic work for the company, her pieces have been well-received by audiences and critics, and her choreographic voice is becoming a leading one in the Dallas/Fort Worth region. Bollinger begins by choosing a theme and then finding music to fit the work. "I start searching for songs. I look for music that I can imagine choreographing to . . . Then as I listen, I can start seeing the dance, the structure of it . . . OK, that sounds like this group coming from this side of the stage, taking over and then right when that change happens boom, it blows open or the girl is being tossed."

"Because what I am saying this time is stronger, more conflicted, raw, the music [of Radiohead] tells a great story." She wanted to create a bold statement, but she also knew she needed a variety of tones. "You can't yell at the audience the whole time; they are going to become numb." She listened to many songs, trying to pick a sequence that would have the right arc for the work she envisioned. She worked to find songs that would guide each section in a separate choreographic direction in order to "give a clear difference from the other sections and what they look like, not the same idea with a different sound behind it."

Bollinger crafts her pieces by choosing music, next working out the overall structure, and then developing specific choreography with the dancers. She does not create much material prior to being with them in the studio. "A lot of choreographers come in with movement. I rarely create a big section on myself . . . I might play with some ideas first, but I like to work in the space with the dancers so it's very fresh. The style of the movement is in my head—sharp or something swirling—but for the actual creation of the steps I like the dancers to be involved."

The four sections of the work move through different moods. In the first section, to the song "$2 + 2 = 5$," "we are angry but still going through the motions [of everyday life] . . . the movement is going from structure to mania." In the second section, she played with the feeling of a chess game. "There's this one moment where all the dancers get rewound back into different formations, everything snapped and gets pulled back. Even though their movements are strong and powerful . . . there are moments when I feel like we are really pawns and are being played with."

The third section is to the song "Paranoid Android." "You get to that place of doubt. How do you find what to believe anymore? That's where the movement breaks open. There is more contact between dancers where they are moving more fluidly and covering space." The last section is more somber and still. "We need the echo of what we speak out now to continue to the next generation . . . [The dancers] are on the ground, their arms are reaching up into the light as they have gone through frustration, anger, battling. They wind up exhausted on the floor but there is still this thread of hope making them reach up." At the end of the piece, the dancers do a novel version of the theater term "breaking the fourth wall." They stand at the back of the stage, beating first their hands and then their heads on the hanging fabric cyclorama. The rhythmic motions create ripples that travel upwards, which in the blue light appear almost like flames. It's an interesting juxtaposition of a classic gesture of futility with the upward movement and creates a beautiful stage picture. As intended, she created something "somber and hopeful."

Without realizing it, for any work she creates, Bollinger starts to picture the costumes as she pictures the movement, or at least the general idea of them, and the lighting as well, as it's "part of the overall shape of the dance." Are the dancers in long skirts? Are the legs exposed? The tones in the music give her a sense of color palette. For this work, she wanted costumes that were "minimalist but modern and sharp . . . held together but pushed apart." And she planned for the same aesthetic to be in the lighting. While she did not use a set designer, the different sections each had different backgrounds—scrim, cyc, and hanging black columns of fabric. "[As I work] I am truly picturing it on stage with lighting and

Dancers in the
opening of the
piece

Dancers in the opening section in a box of light

background . . . the second section is supposed to look like a chess board. The spacing of where the dancers walk out had to be very specific because they have to fit into a square of light and the backdrop is going to have three . . . dark panels to look like the chessboard continued vertically."

Bollinger recalls that she was thinking of a dark palette for the costumes, but it was costume designer John Ahrens who suggested gray rather than navy or black because he wanted to be able to do a variety of textures and tones. Ahrens, resident costume designer for Bruce Wood Dance, remembers suggesting a dark palette for the grays rather than a paler tone partially because in addition to designing each piece, he wanted to balance the concert's overall look. He was already well into designing the other major work in the concert, by a guest artist, and they had agreed upon light blue-gray costumes.

Costume designer John Ahrens has a decades-long history with Bruce Wood Dance and has worked with Bollinger several times as a designer for her choreography. He knew that her development process was lengthy, and that on their previous collaboration, it had taken her a long time to be able to finalize what she wanted. Since Ahrens had to be sure there would be time to build these costumes, and the rest of the pieces in the concert as well, he had to push her to begin discussions about the details of the costume design. Although her choreography was still in process, and had not been edited into the final version, she had created plenty of movement for him to respond to.

"I just like dancers. . . . and I find choreographers generally pretty easy to deal with." Ahrens is able to nudge a choreographer forward, helping to put pieces together into a whole. He began his career in New York, where working under the famed costumer Betty Williams, he helped to create costumes for most of the leading modern dance companies. He learned from Williams about collaboration with dancers and choreographers, how best to communicate and how to navigate the timeline of the creative process.

"There are moments in the dance when the dancers are being tossed or thrown around or manipulated by something bigger than them. But at the same time, their movements are sharp. They don't look fragile—they look like they are pushing up against something and battling it, at war with it even," Bollinger explains. Over conversations with Ahrens, she started to gravitate to what she described as "the idea of structure coming undone or being deconstructed." They talked about the general feeling the clothes should have and decided on sleeveless short dresses for the women and bare chests and pants

for the men, everyone half-exposed and half-covered. Bollinger had a strong sense of what she wanted for the piece: "Modern and contemporary but raw, not sleek." Ahrens recalls that "Joy and I traded little sketches together . . . sometimes pushing the notebook back and forth."

However, it was not until she came across images from a collection by fashion designer Gareth Pugh, and sent Ahrens a photo, that they were able to resolve the design. Some visual ideas in the photo communicated how she wanted the costumes to feel more clearly than she had previously been able to explain to Ahrens. The fashion image had strong shoulders and angular pieces of fabric seamed together into a striking, body-hugging gown. They borrowed the idea of geometric patchwork and the sharp silhouette, putting the seams on the outside to give a rawness and sense of deconstruction. Ahrens took influence from the Pugh dress, but designed a different overall shape and his own geometry for the fabric collage. The designer mentions, and Bollinger is keenly aware, that she needs to see a prototype to be sure how she feels about a costume design idea. He made a couple of variations in a fabric he had in the studio, and once they had a version of the patchworked dress shape agreed upon, Ahrens then designed sleek fitted pants for the men that would coordinate with the dresses, using geometric pieced shapes to create a similar aesthetic.

Ahrens had a shopper in New York send him samples of gray knit fabrics and seeing them inspired him. "They were just beautiful stuff and I got really excited when I saw them," said the designer. He worked out a plan using five separate textures of fabrics, arranged differently for each dancer. The bottom hems of the dresses were left purposely uneven.

As the piece progressed, they had to figure out some logistics of the dance: How tight did the dresses need to be so that the men could securely lift the women? Where on the men's torsos should the top edge of the pants be to best grip the body and stay up, and also to give the dancers a flattering proportion? Additionally, there was an issue when the company started rehearsing with the men bare-chested. Their sweat interfered with a lot of the lifts as they partnered the women. The choreographer asked the designer for help. As they have worked together for 16 years, Ahrens was comfortable talking to her firmly and directly. He knew she had learned much from Bruce Wood, a mentor to both of them. But he also knew that "she worries a lot," so he didn't want to be snappy with her. And so, as he tells it "I looked her right in the eye and said 'Joy, you wanted

Olivia Davis and Seth York

them bare-chested. You fix it.' And she . . . solved the problem." He added "What I wanted to tell her, although I knew I couldn't, was 'What would Bruce do?' Bruce would either fix it or say, 'I can do it [in these costumes] and if I can do it you can do it.'" Bollinger's solution was to add flesh-toned socks for the women in the second section so they wouldn't slip against their partners' bodies. But they stayed barefoot for the opening section to give them traction for the thrashing and jumps.

Ahrens also costumes debutante competitions in Texas, and so he is very comfortable doing complicated and elaborate styles. However, over time he has come to realize that for dance, simpler is usually the best solution: "you don't want to get in the way of a dancer moving through space." Between the prototype and the final version for *In My Your Head*, Ahrens made the patchwork pieces larger and more graphic. "You get these crazy ideas and then go back to the beginning and figure out the simplest thing we can do and it's the most successful. And I keep having to relearn this." In the end, designer and choreographer were satisfied that the costumes helped to show the dancers' strength in the uncertain landscape, coming through frustration and anger to a solemn hope.

Dancers in silhouette

Dancers in the "chessboard" section of the dance

2

Styles and Genres of Concert Dance Costume

When planning a dance costume, it can be helpful to break types of costume into genres. This provides a shorthand for communication between designers and choreographers. Additionally, recognizing the genres will help to understand both contemporary trends and past traditions. While not all artists would use the exact same categories, and terminology varies across the industry, the terms presented here represent the kinds of genres used. Whether deciding to follow tradition or break with it, it helps to base decisions on historical context. Types of garments worn for dance are associated with specific styles of dance, and also with different movements and trends within contemporary and modern dance. If a contemporary choreographer's style is linked to a past one, their costume preference may follow suit. A follower of Martha Graham's technique might want a skirt with a weighty flow to it, to ensure a strong geometry reads from an *arabesque*.

Any genre of dance costume may also conform to the fashion taste of the time in terms of preferences for colors or silhouettes, even if adapted for dance. While wider pants are in style, choreographers may want gauchos, and then when tastes switch to narrower pants, the norm becomes leggings and joggers. The dance world also has its own unique fashion trends. Different eras prefer dancing in bare feet vs using socks, or unitards vs a tight tank and leggings combo. Former dancer turned costume designer Elena Comendador is not a big fan of the current urge to dance in socks. She stated, "I'm of another generation of dancers. I know my aesthetic is different. I

Jody Sperling of Time Lapse Dance performing her own choreography in *Ice Cycle* (for more detail see Case Study #5)

have to remind myself I am living in a millennial world, and my eye has to get used to these different types of looks now."

Just like with fashion, a generation may want to react against their elders. Choreographer Liz Gerring stated that "I would never put my dancers in unitards like Merce Cunningham, it feels old fashioned now, especially the scoop neck, but it worked perfectly for his work." Minimalism gives birth to maximalism—those who started out in the profession when unitards were practically a modern dance uniform now might create their own work using boldly theatrical styles. Of course, history and tradition do not have to determine the choices available to clothe dancers for any given project. And many projects may synthesize, combine or deconstruct several of these categories. Even in this book's attempt to break the costumes into categories, genres will overlap or duplicate somewhat.

TRADITIONAL DANCE COSTUME

Many choreographers today choose to use the traditional costume associated with the type of dance they do. This can vary from those who strive to truly follow historical practices to those who work within a traditional framework, but with some modernization. However, even the most historically based pieces likely use costumes made from readily available fabrics that echo but do not exactly reproduce those from centuries earlier. Dyes, fibers and technology provide different options. Traditional ballet companies do not use the silk tights of the nineteenth century, and practitioners of Indian classical dance buy garments sewn into pants, rather than pleating and wrapping long lengths of fabric around their legs every time they perform.

Most traditional concert dance forms predate the era when theatrical design became a separate artistic practice. Performance outfits from earlier times echo the clothing worn by the people of that era and culture, adapted for either theatrical entertainment or religious ritual. Traditional dance costumes start from the clothing vocabulary of the culture, but are then modified to create an interesting spectacle, foster storytelling and accentuate and accommodate the movements of the dance.

Classical Indian Dance

Classical Indian dance is a traditional style that is still widely practiced today. Like with ballet, practitioners study the classical technique, and then create their own works that adhere to the movements and aesthetics of the form. There are eight different styles of classical Indian dance. For Bharatanatyam and Kuchipudi, the two styles discussed in this section, the women's costumes are fairly similar. The top of the costumes resembles a sari, but more fitted. Fabric is draped into a one-shouldered top over a short-sleeved fitted top like the ones worn under saris. The pants are pleated and draped, full at the top and tapering towards the ankle. The hip area is defined by a more fitted wrapped piece that curves up towards the front, where an apron-like pleated fan of the same fabric fills the space between the legs. The selections vary in cut, color and sleeve length, and the fabrics can have many different styles of borders and prints. The waist is set off by a belt, and the dancers also wear a variety of jewelry including bracelets, necklaces and hair ornaments. Importantly, they wear cuffs of bells at the ankle that provide musical accent to their movements.

Classical Indian dances were first done in Hindu temples around 2,000 years ago.[1] The costume was originally a pleated sari, accented by lots of jewelry, including in the hair. According to Anuradha Nehru of Kalanidhi Dance, the elaborate costumes served to enhance the splendor of the dancers. "The beauty of the dancers was very important, in the aesthetic of the day . . . the dances used to be danced in the temples, in praise of gods. After that, they moved into courts, but always done for some sort of patron." The costumes gradually evolved into the draped pants worn today. Ranee Ramaswamy of Ragamala Dance Company explained that when dancing in a sari, "it's difficult to put it on and to keep it in place and make it look good. So that's how the costume evolved. Over the years, costumes have been more baggy, more draped, [or tailored with] pleats on the sides." While at first the length of sari fabric was wound around the legs like pants, the more modern version is permanently sewn that way, while preserving the pleats and draping that simulate the original effect. Hooks were first used to fasten and unfasten the various parts, although some modern innovators save time by using Velcro instead.

Ranee Ramaswamy—Ragamala Dance Company

Ranee Ramaswamy and her company Ragamala Dance Company, which she co-directs with her daughter Aparna Ramaswamy, perform the classical dance style of India called Bharatanatyam, but their works are not purely traditional. Their recent work, *Written in Water*, uses projections on the floor and on scrims behind the stage, and incorporates not only Indian music but also jazz and Iraqi music.

Bharatanatyam started in the temples of southern India and is considered the oldest form of Indian classical dance. The movements are very specific and include nuanced positions for the whole body, including hands, fingers, eyes and head. Each of the eight forms has its own style of gesture and uses rhythm differently.[2] Ramaswamy explains that while the practice is traditional, contemporary artists each create their own works, they are not performing dances from the past. "Bharatanatyam is a language . . . a very poetic, metaphorical language. It doesn't work if you talk about hospitals or a train running . . . [Ragamala Dance] creates evening-length work that comes from the ideas that we bring to the table. Then comes the music, then comes the dance, then comes the production." Lately, the company's themes have been less contemporary and "more back into myth. [However], the more back you go, it seems to be more contemporary." Ramaswamy feels that traditional costumes best suit the metaphorical nature of the dance and allow the dancers to become timeless storytellers. "We are removed from who we are every day and become these mysterious beings. The people wearing [the costume] are not ancient people, we are everyday people."

Ramaswamy had a period in her career when she experimented with combining Bharatanatyam with other forms of dance, although without crossing over. She worked with other dancers in her home of Minneapolis, ranging from ballet to flamenco to African dance. She sought to find out "what was the ability of this old style to meet with other cultures?" She collaborated with a costume designer to come up with costumes that bridged the two worlds. Her favorite costume from the experiments was for a work danced in collaboration with a Japanese taiko drummer. "It suited that piece and was very freeing," Ramaswamy recalled. The costume, which she found very elegant, was reminiscent of a kimono but adapted into a skirt shape that gave dancers plenty of room to do the half-sitting position so key to Bharatanatyam. The Japanese print fabrics of their costumes linked the musicians and dancers. "What we wear has to mirror the music and where we are. If we wear our traditional costume and dance to taiko drumming, it won't match."

While Ramaswamy noted that the crossover costumes were easy to dance in and didn't require three hours to get dressed the way the south Indian ones do, she decided to return to tradition. She recounted when her daughter Aparna, now her co-artistic director, returned from college and said, "'mom we should go back to our traditional costume—it suits us the best and accentuates every movement that we do.' . . . It took a ten-year period to see how that costume fit our body and did service to the style we were doing." While they still collaborate with poets and musicians from other cultures, they always also use an Indian orchestra. Rather than having "a middle place where you belong to two worlds . . . now we establish the Indian world first . . . bringing another culture into our world. Now it works perfectly that we are wearing our costumes."

Anuradha Nehru—Kalanidhi Dance

Anuradha Nehru began her dance training in Bharatanatyam in her native India. Thirty years ago, it was the most popular style, and so there were more teachers available. She switched to the Kuchipudi style only by chance. When she went to college, the only teacher she could find taught Kuchipudi. But the switch was fortuitous, and it heightened her enthusiasm for dance. She "fell in love when she switched to the Kuchipudi style, as it was more fluid than Bharatanatyam." She later moved to the United States and founded Kalanidhi Dance as a school and then a dance company over two decades ago in Maryland.

Like Ramaswamy, Nehru also believes that the traditional costume is essential to performing the dance: "The fact that we dance barefoot is because of how rhythmic the form is, and the contact with the earth is so important. We beat out complex rhythms with our feet and wear bells on our ankles." She also believes that the pants and apron-like fan are closely tied to the style of leg movement. The half-sitting posture, "like a deep *plié*," is the base position for much of the choreography. "The fan is very flattering to the look. A lot of the leg movements create a certain geometry: triangles and semi circles that you create in space, and the *plié* creates a diamond that we fill with the fan." She points out that the hip position is also very important to the choreography. The way the costume hugs the hips helps the nuances in the movement to show, as well as making the overall effect more aesthetically pleasing.

Nehru's work for Kalanidhi Dance uses classic Hindu stories, but she also created a piece based on personal stories from the dancers in her company, and recently did a work about climate change, filtered through an Indian philosophical lens. Most of her accompaniment is Indian, but she has incorporated poetry and songs from other cultures as well. Nehru has brought her expertise in Kuchipudi to other forms and has been a consultant and collaborator for theater and opera. She collaborated on several works with Opera Lafayette, putting Kuchipudi choreography to Baroque music. "The only vocabulary I know is the Indian classical, but it's interesting how it lends itself to opera music or more contemporary themes. A lot of the operas we have worked on are eighteenth- and nineteenth-century librettos, but reinterpreted."

For Opera Lafayette, Nehru directed and choreographed *La Forêt Enchantée* (*The Enchanted Forest*) with music by Francesco Geminiani. The work was a ballet pantomime, a common form in the Baroque era. The original story was about the Crusades. Instead they chose to set it in India during the Mughal invasion, which

Shyama Iyer of Guru Vandana Arts Academy performs the Bharathanatyam style of Indian classical dance

Lekha Reddy waits for her cue

paralleled the Crusaders attacking the Jews. The male characters were Mughal, and they wore the full-skirted tops and narrow pants of the historical time. Nehru worked with costume designer Mariam Barri to adapt the usual Kuchipudi costumes for the female Kalanidhi dancers, who portrayed spirits. They used ivory fabrics for the clothing and added ethereal wire and fabric headdresses with lightweight sheer veils trailing down the back. She adapted her traditional choreography to suit the characters the men played. "I made the male dancers more theatrical and less dancey . . . Mughal costumes are not meant for South Indian dance, so I had to change the movement to suit the male dancers. If they had too many leaps and intricate footwork, it would not suit the characters and the play."

Traditional Ballet

Within the Western world that produced the dance forms that make up most of the content of this book, the most common European traditional dance form still being practiced is ballet. While many current ballets are in contemporary or neoclassical genres with updated clothing conventions, plenty of ballets still choose a traditional look. Ballet originated in Europe as court entertainment at the end of the 1500s. Our current traditional ballet costumes are based on styles that evolved and then solidified in the nineteenth century. Both men and women wear flat ballet slippers, and women most commonly wear satin pointe shoes. Women and men usually match the color of the tights to the color of the shoes. The default color of tights and shoes for women has been the pale peachy-pink dubbed "ballet pink" referencing but not exactly copying a Caucasian flesh tone. As women of color have joined ballet companies, this standard is evolving to instead put each dancer in tights and shoes close to her own skin tone.

The "romantic" tutu silhouette still used today originated in the 1830s. The shape of the bodice and skirt comes from the clothing of the 1830s and 40s. Women wear a stiff, fitted bodice, with a V-shaped point at the waist, structured with boning, and a full bell-shaped skirt made of lightweight fabric, usually tulle, that extends well past the knee in length. Arms are sometimes bare, but often have a short lightweight sleeve that sits off the shoulder. Hair is worn up in a bun and is often ornamented with a tiara or other small headpiece. The shape of the bodice did not change much, but towards the end of the century skirts became shorter, first to the bell tutu seen in many Degas paintings, and then shorter still, and flatter

to show more leg. This last shape, known as a classical tutu, is the silhouette a modern audience pictures when they think of a ballerina. The classical tutu is made of layers of netting built up from the lower hip to support the flat skirt on top. The top layer can be any type of fabric, accented with a broad array of decoration. Current ballet companies use all three of these shapes. Common names for variations on the classical tutu include platter tutus, pancake tutus and powderpuff tutus.

Men's traditional ballet costume features heavyweight footed tights worn as pants, with a structured dance belt smoothing out the anatomy in the crotch area. Men's tights are not flesh-toned. Instead they are commonly pale or black although they can also be more vibrant colors. The color of the shoe is matched to the color of the tights in most cases. The top half is either a doublet or a sleeveless doublet with a shirt underneath. A doublet is a fitted, structured garment with long sleeves, ending just past the waist. The front waist usually angles into a V-shape, elongating the torso in the same manner as the women's bodice. The shirts are loosely fit around the arms, but made of a flowing, drapey fabric so the body shape is still easily apparent. This shirt is consistent with actual men's shirts during the centuries when ballet costume originated.

In ballet, the structured costumes do allow the torso to arch and bend, but since the arms and legs are the primary focus of most of the choreography, the limbs have the widest range of movement. The shorter tutus give greater emphasis to the women's legs, as they allow the audience to see more. Men often hold women at the waist, to lift them and to support them during turns, so added decoration is usually concentrated at the chest area of the bodice. The waist is kept free of anything that will interfere with a secure grip or be damaged by abrasion from the partner's hands. The tight structured bodice ensures that when the dancer is lifted, there is no turning or slipping—she and the costume move as one.

Overall the costumes are designed to show the ethereal elegance of the female performers and the solid but graceful muscularity of the men. Principals and soloists wear costumes that make them more noticeable. The corps are purposely dressed identically in most cases, allowing them to function as one unit, rather than any highlighting of individuality both in terms of the choreography and the visual look. Story ballet costumes vary depending on the character being portrayed and the overall setting for the piece. Traditional ballet costumes are commonly used in both story ballets and in more abstract ballets that focus on movement to music.

West African Dance

Iddrisu Saaka—Traditional Dance of Ghana

Iddrisu Saaka teaches traditional dance styles of West Africa at Wesleyan University, where he is Associate Professor of the Practice in Dance. Saaka began his study of dance as a child in Northern Ghana. "In the villages in Ghana, music and dance are part of the daily life of the people. In my village, at every important occasion, there is always music and dance." The children watch the adults perform at festivals, naming ceremonies and weddings. Once they understand the basics, they join the performances.

For many of the dances he teaches, traditional costumes play an essential role. The Damba dance from Northern Ghana, which is part of the Damba festival marking the naming ceremony of the prophet Muhammad, is traditionally performed by chiefs or royals. The dancers wear clothing based on a style from that region. The tops are loose smocks, ending above the knee, made of striped "Gonja cloth."[3] The wide-shouldered smock's upper half is made of densely packed vertical pleats. The pleats release below the chest, creating a fuller skirt-like section in the lower half. The round neckline is slit at the front and embellished with embroidery that coordinates with the blue, black and white of the stripes. Underneath, the dancers wear traditional loose pants with a dropped crotch. For the Damba dance, the smocks are looser and fuller than the everyday life version. "It is supposed to be a rare dance. When the people are dancing, they twirl so the outfit creates designs in space," Saaka explained. "Without these [costumes] it won't make sense. The outfit supports the movement." According to Saaka, the outfit became very popular throughout Ghana, and "people not even connected to the culture wear it now."

Many Ghanaian dances rely on costume, but both the costumes and the dances themselves vary widely. Another dance Saaka teaches is the Bamaya dance. The origins of dances come down through oral traditions, and so explanations vary. When Saaka tells the story for the Bamaya dance, he explains that it was created in an attempt to rid the land of drought. The people prayed and fasted and finally learned that the drought was imposed as punishment because the men were mistreating the women. "The men had to pacify the gods. One way to do that was to dress up as women and go to the market in the center of town and dance. It was a humiliation. The people saw them and made fun and hooted. Then they made a dance from it." The dancers wear skirts and sometimes even makeup and fake breasts. The dance uses a lot of movement at the waist, and a belt covered with tassels of beads that rattle as the dancers' hips tilt and

shake is essential to its performance. The beads add to the percussion of the dance, as well as highlighting the feminine form.

Some of the costume choices are purely practical. Since Northern Ghana is very hot, men often remove their shirts to pick up a cool breeze. However, this is only practiced with dances meant for entertainment. Saaka said that "for Damba, being royal, it would be sacrilegious for a royal to take off their shirt in public." Some practitioners of traditional Ghanaian dance choose customary outfits, whether for storytelling, to enhance the movement or to preserve their traditional culture. However, many of the dances are not as tied to specific clothing and, especially if dances are performed on stages in cities, Saaka noted that dancers select clothing purely for looks, to impress their audiences. And of course, "they are influenced by the outside world." Even revered traditional dances may be performed with flashier costumes, or shirtless, for tourists or to attract attention. As with any culture, some practitioners criticize the deviation, and get upset when they feel that their culture is misrepresented.

When he teaches college courses in West African dance, "I teach them from my own perspective. I have to choreograph the dances, [but] they are closer to what people call traditional." He directs the West African Drumming and Dance Concert at the end of each semester, and for these performances, he buys Ghanaian clothing from Africa, or commissions a local Ghanaian seamstress familiar with the clothing styles to build traditional garments. Saaka also created a touring performance for elementary schools that teaches the cultures of West Africa by combining music, dance and storytelling. For this he wears what he termed his "own style of West African clothing, similar to the costume you will find in professional dance companies in West Africa." He wears very wide and full drawstring pants and a loose sleeveless shirt made from African fabrics. The shirt is open at the sides—narrow bands of fabric hold the front and back together. The shirt keeps the dancer cool in hot weather, and loose clothing is essential to performing the movement. "I used to dance with regular pants, and I would rip them," he recalled with a wry grin. He chooses this clothing to educate his audience, and because "it connects me to the culture."

Saaka also creates his own choreography for professional performances. For these, he uses "contemporary techniques, but influenced by my background as a West African dancer. I use West African aesthetics to inform what I do." A recent piece called *Relation*, where he interacts with a Ghanaian drum, an *atsimevu*,

Dancer G.D Harris of Dayton Contemporary Dance Company performs a restaging of Asadata Dafora's 1932 work *Awassa Astrige/Ostrich*. Costume Design by Catti. Dafora, born in Sierra Leone, was one of the first Black choreographers to bring African dance to the concert stage in the United States.

used African dance music. But the dance itself was not traditional at all, and he used the tall cylindrical drum almost like a dance partner. While lying on his back, he put his feet into the opening, and slowly arced his newly giant "leg" from side to side. Later, he balanced the drum on his head, and wowed the audience as he danced without dislodging it. For works like this, he bases his costume on "how I feel in the outfit." He usually just wears simple contemporary clothing like T-shirts and track pants. For some works, he wears the traditional full African pants, but paired with a T-shirt.

Enslaved people in the Americas brought traditions from their African homeland. One of these, the vital tradition of dance, provided a common ground and means of expression that straddled language barriers between different peoples.[4] Jazz and tap and other contemporary dance forms developed from earlier African American styles, which in turn evolved from African dances. However, the costumes used in both twentieth- and twenty-first-century jazz and tap performance usually follow other styles, like pedestrian, theatrical or lyrical.

UPDATED AND TRANSLATED TRADITIONAL

While there is, of course, a gradual continuum from a truly traditional costume to a translated one, there comes a point where the goal is to not just evolve but consciously alter a traditional clothing shape. The two most common ways to update traditional looks are to pare down and streamline, as simplicity tends to feel more modern, or to combine traditional costume shapes with streetwear or fashion influence.

Countless ballet costumes have been designed as updated or translated takes on the tutu. From punk-inspired jagged crinolines to fashion designer Iris van Herpen's armor-like tutus constructed from segments of plastic and laser-cut metal, the iconic tutu has provided fodder for commentary and transformation. Other traditional styles are also frequently adapted for concert dance. A Caribbean costume can be translated for contemporary concert dance by using the traditional full-tiered skirt but keeping the whole group in a monochromatic color scheme or switching loose blouses to contemporary stretch tops. Anthropologist and choreographer Dr. Pearl Primus adapted African costumes for her concert dance performances in the 1950s, following traditional styles, but with more tailored tops and simpler decoration than the originals.

Sandra Woodall—*Classical Symphony* with Yuri Possokhov at San Francisco Ballet (Premiere 2010)

Costume designer Sandra Woodall's work ranges from contemporary dance to classical ballet, and she strives to form a personal connection with any piece she works on. "One of the things I love to do, even with classical dance, is to take a garment and create a new way to have it work, of handling it." She designed *Classical Symphony* for San Francisco Ballet, choreographed by her frequent collaborator Yuri Possokhov. The choreographer wanted his version of the piece to be an exploration of the classical form. While his impetus to create the work was his training at the Bolshoi Ballet, he sought to make an homage, not a replication, and so he wanted it to have a contemporary look. Woodall took her own version of the same artistic journey and tried to really study the tutu and its relation to the dancer's body. What was essential and what was superfluous about the form? She drew the conclusion that "the choreography is based on having the line that cuts across the body at the level of the tutu. That was very interesting. For the men I tried to explore what is the male dancer's version of that, the element that needs that flexibility? I think it's the relation of the arm to the body. It's one they struggle with, as a doublet can be restricting and masks the relation of the arm and the body."

Woodall created costumes that keep the lines of classical male and female ballet costumes but are very pared down. The color palette is timeless—the women in a rich golden hue, ornamented in black and white, and men in black accented with white and gold. The women wear leotards that echo a ballet bodice—the top appears to end just above the bust, edged with a thin contrasting dark line. Skin-toned mesh over the shoulders in fact supports the bodice. Two layers of gossamer-thin fabric form the skirt, the underlayer ruched to give it texture reminiscent of the radial pleats of a traditional tutu. Flexible hoops sewn into the edge hold the flat circles taut. The top layer is embellished with scrollwork, hand-painted to remain light and semi-transparent. The female dancers' legs stay bare although they wear classic pink satin pointe shoes. The men wear doublets that follow the traditional shape, although like the women they are made in stretch fabric that forms to the body without needing much structure. A rectangular section of grid-like graphic black mesh replaces the shoulder area. The torso and arms remain visually separate units but are also linked. The center front of the doublet is white with painted gold scrollwork that echoes the women's costume. The men's outfits are otherwise black and sleek from shoulder to foot, finished off with matching slippers and tights.

MINIMALISM AND ABSTRACTION

Modern dance began in the early twentieth century, and just like much of the other art of the time—whether music, visual art or architecture—a clean, simple aesthetic was favored. In dance, minimalism allowed the focus to be on the body and the choreography. Martha Graham's work became nearly synonymous with the long, full skirts that intensified her weighty movements. Similar dresses, usually body-conscious and stretchy in the torso area, but flowing in the skirt, are found in works by many of the seminal choreographers of the mid-twentieth century, from José Limón to Alvin Ailey. The corresponding menswear look is simple shapes in knit fabrics—tailored or slightly flowing pants and shirts. These clothing shapes follow the general clothing shape favored in the 1930s and 40s for men and women. However, the look is pared down—no pockets, no buttons, no collars. The lack of standard clothing detail keeps the shapes abstracted. The opening section of Ailey's famous 1960 work *Revelations* is grounded by the earth-toned flaring dresses and pants that help to turn the dancers' sweeping gestures into sculptural shapes.

This flowing look has endured, and the term "lyrical" is often used for current versions of this style. Many choreographers favor simple clothing shapes without too much detail which can be in either light or heavy fabrics that flow or drape on the dancer. Shapes may skim the body or be quite voluminous. Twenty-first-century abstract costumes may be gendered or unisex, with skirts or pants an option for any dancer. Bare legs, the feet either barefoot or with simple slippers in skin tones, usually accompany this look.

The next phase of the minimal look that evolved during the twentieth century was even more focused on the body, covering all or part of it tightly in stretch fabric. Leotards and unitards form the base of this look, which can be colored, painted and decorated in all kinds of ways. Leotards are one-piece garments incorporating briefs and a top, with or without sleeves. Unitards are similar one-piece garments that cover the torso and also all or part of the leg, sleeves optional. Unitards that stop at the thigh are currently often referred to as biketards. These types of garments can put focus on the shape of the body unadorned or become a way to decorate the body with color and pattern, while still allowing the viewer to see the dancer's every gesture. These styles became common from the 1930s on. Although it started earlier, the narrow look parallels the clothing of the 1950s and 60s and became more prevalent in that time. In the later 1950s and early 1960s, pants for both men and women had a narrow silhouette, and both sexes wore tight knit tops for casual looks—for men, tight turtlenecks or polo shirts, for women, sweaters, tops, etc. Pants had become more common for women in contemporary clothing by this time, so a more unisex look onstage fit with what was happening offstage. This style of costume allowed the whole body to be seen, and rather than flowing fabric, the focus came to angles and nuances of the torso and limbs. The stark geometry suited choreographers like Merce Cunningham. For his 1958 work *Summerspace*, the dancers wore unitards designed by artist Robert Rauschenberg painted with pointillistic spots that echoed the look of his abstract painted backdrop.

These genres most typically are danced barefoot and without tights or socks. Plenty of current dances are still performed in unitards, while other choreographers find them too linked to the last generation and prefer tight-fitting two-piece looks: tanks paired with leggings or bike shorts. Even if the whole look is monochromatic and sleek, a line at the high hip where the two garments meet breaks the flat surface.

A simple costume can require a lot of decisions. Costume designer Holly Hynes described a typical conversation with choreographers when she works on modern ballet. "They might say to me 'I don't want them to look like they have any clothing on, but obviously we can't do that. I want to get away with as little clothing as possible. I want to see their muscles, the line of the leg.' Then you are probably talking milliskin (a spandex fabric). But are we talking painted or ombre-d or dyed? White or black or gray? There are basic questions you throw out in that early conversation and then you go away and dream up where the seams are, where the lines are."

Liz Vandal—*24 Preludes by Chopin* by Marie Chouinard for Compagnie Marie Chouinard (Premiere 1999)

Achieving the ultimate simplicity, perfectly in line with the spirit of a piece, can be a challenging task for a designer. Costume designer Liz Vandal has designed a wide range of works for companies that range from ballet and contemporary dance to Cirque du Soleil. While she has created many elaborate, intricate costumes, *24 Preludes by Chopin* for Compagnie Marie Chouinard stands out as one of her favorites from her career. "I think it was the most beautiful thing I've done, and one of the simplest." She put the women in sheer black leotards, and the men in black shorts, both accented with narrow rectangles of vinyl. The piano that was on stage with the dancers inspired her design. "I wanted to find that black vinyl look, but I didn't want to make a catsuit, so I put a line on the breast going all around. And another line on the pubic and hiding the butt crack . . . and it's the same black shininess of the keys." The men also have a line of black vinyl looping through the legs on the shorts. And, all the dancers wear a black brush-like headpiece, arcing along the head like a Greek helmet or the crest of a bird. "The dancers came on stage and they looked simple and pure, and it was enough. When they waved their bodies, these lines were just part of them."

REHEARSAL-BASED

Choreographers watch their dancers daily in rehearsal clothing, and sometimes this becomes their preferred aesthetic. George Balanchine created many traditional ballets performed in tutus and doublets, but he also desired a starker look for his more contemporary creations. The works, which are now known as his "black and white ballets" feature men in fitted white T-shirts, black tights and white socks and ballet shoes, and women in simple black tank leotards with pale pink tights and shoes. The earliest of these, *The Four Temperaments*, was first performed in 'practice clothes' in 1951. (An earlier version that premiered in 1946 had elaborate costumes.)[5] These minimalist costumes suited the spare modern music of composers like Hindemith and Stravinsky and allowed the dances to feel much more abstract while still ballet and not modern dance.

Although styles change, the trend of having dancers perform in rehearsal clothing has endured. The 1970s and 80s trend, exemplified by *A Chorus Line,* had dancers in leotards and leg warmers. Many current choreographers like both the aesthetics and the functional properties of contemporary athleisure wear and have their designers translate workout clothes for the stage. The effect created can be abstract—simple shapes in subtle colors that let the body take focus, or it can emphasize the idea of the dancers as dancers, performing as themselves rather than playing characters or representing abstractions. Rehearsal clothing can create an ungendered look with simple tank tops and bike shorts or emphasize different genders with bra tops and compression T-shirts. Dancers are athletes, and the wicking properties and exceptional degree of stretch and rebound in workout wear helps them to perform at their best. Additionally, the casual chic of the style appeals to those both on and off stage. Athleisure wear has spread from the workout studio to the grocery store and lunch dates. And this present-day trend of leggings, strappy tanks and bra tops, sturdy T-shirts, joggers and bike shorts is also seen in performance.

Liz Gerring—*Glacier* for Liz Gerring Dance (Premiere 2013)

Choreographer Liz Gerring developed *Glacier* from a series of hand and arm gestures, which then progressed into full body movements. The music for the work originated during a visit to Glacier Lake in Colorado. The composer, her frequent collaborator Michael J. Schumacher, collected sounds from nature and combined them with musical instruments to create an installation work, which then became the basis for Gerring's dance. The choreographer explained the aesthetic she prefers for her work: "There is a non-theatricality to what I do." She views her pieces as more of an installation in an art gallery than standard concert dance, and her choreography is very athletic. "Typical dance costumes are not right for this. Everything is very physical—there are sweat issues." Gerring asked costume designer Márion Talán for whites and grays, and for a look where the lines of the dancers' bodies would read well to the audience, without distractions.

The choreographer knew that achieving a unique performance look with a "forward design feeling" from this basic aesthetic would be challenging. Leotards and tights remind Gerring of childhood ballet class, but "I don't want them to look like they are going to yoga class either." Talán used a similar vocabulary to what the dancers wore in rehearsal—shorts, leggings, sometimes a looser top—to create a different look for each of the eight dancers. Some had long sleeves, some shorter and some were in tanks. Bottoms varied from shorts to slim pants to leggings. Each dancer's outfit was two pieces in two different colors: white and gray, gray and black. The look stayed very simple, and to the untrained eye felt un-designed. But, the cut across the dancers' hips where the top and bottom color meet echoed the broad gray rectangle of scrim along the back wall that was set off by the deep black curtain behind it.

PEDESTRIAN OR STREETWEAR

The idea of putting dancers in costumes that resemble everyday clothing is an idea that has been around as long as dancing. Some in the industry call this pedestrian clothing, others real clothes or streetwear. As discussed previously, traditional dance costume forms took inspiration from clothing of their time and place, and many modern and contemporary choreographers also want to see the dancers in something that feels like "real" clothes. This can mean using clothing from the present day or from an older time. And the degree of realism can range from actual off-the-rack clothing, new or vintage, to costumes with a feeling of real clothes but translated into a dance costume version. Historical influences might be used to a fair degree of accuracy or just as inspiration or seasoning. Some choreography may be possible in more structured real clothing, while other works may necessitate adaptations. Evoking a time period rather than replicating it can also be a design choice rather than a logistical one. Using pedestrian clothing for a piece can suggest a time, a place or a subgroup of society. The goal can be to aid in communicating themes or storytelling, or to create a mood or impression.

Nicole Haskins

Choreographer Nicole Haskins stresses humanism in her ballets and wants an aesthetic for her costumes that helps to underscore that. "I try in my choreography to have dancers look and act like people and not be statues or mannequins. Ballet can be very pose-y, if the movement is not embedded from the beginning. Costume can help to give that sense of movement and energy and personhood." She feels that if dancers wear leotards and tights, "it's harder for them to break out of that 'dancer' feeling. With my choreography I try to take advantage of all the training and technique and skills the dancers have, but make it look as spontaneous and natural as possible and not like we have been rehearsing it forever." While she likes costume designers to create new looks for her pieces rather than to copy or simply purchase current clothing, she defines the streetwear aesthetic as successful "if the dancer had to walk outside and do something, they would not look completely out of place."

Kyle Abraham and Karen Young—*The Gettin'* for Abraham in Motion (Premiere 2014)

When Kyle Abraham conceived of *The Gettin'*, inspired by the 1960s civil rights movement, bringing out the time period with the clothing was in his plan at the outset. The piece was inspired by events in South Africa in the early 1960s and set to jazz music from Max Roach's *Freedom Now Suite* written in that era about the struggle in both the United States and Africa.

Costume designer Karen Young explained how the costumes fit into the overall vision for the work. The creative team strove for "a loose reference to that period. The music took us there, but the set was contemporary." Projections of black and white graphic imagery created a backdrop for the dancers. Text and images layered together illustrated the themes of the work rather than creating scenery. Young explained that she and Abraham sought to suggest

the clothing of the era but did not worry about the clothing being specific to South Africa. Young used clothing shapes popular everywhere in 1960, but built the women's dresses from African fabrics, although the textiles were in fact West African rather than from South Africa. She put the women "in dresses with full skirts [creating] the period shape, but also a bit contemporary as well." While she used modern button-down shirts for the men, she didn't use stretch fabrics so that "the fit felt like that time." The men in narrow trousers and slim-cut short-sleeved shirts move fluently with the women in boat-necked dresses. The colors and patterns of the costumes formed a harmonious whole, and each dancer had their own individual look. While the costumes showed the lines of the body and flowed with the movement, they could easily have been from a play or movie. The dancers wore socks and jazz shoes, adding to the 'regular clothes' feel, whereas the majority of Abraham's other works for his company are done barefoot.

THEATRICAL

Theatrical dance costumes are usually based on pedestrian clothing but heightened or translated into a more stylized version. In this category, the purpose of the costume is not only to help to convey the meaning of an overall dance, but also to portray a character with a specific personality or narrative function. The costumes, together with other design elements like lighting, and sometimes scenery, projections or props, help to create a whole environment for the dance. Theatrical dance costume as used here does not mean costumes for dancers in musicals. The actual costumes used in a musical are not inherently different from those used in concert dance. However, musicals are outside the scope of this book because the conversation during the design process is so different; it tends to center on the script. The performers speak dialog and sing lyrics, which means that movement is not the primary mode of communication with the audience. However, because of the association of jazz and tap with musicals, costumes used for some styles of jazz and tap concert pieces tend to follow this aesthetic even if there is minimal narrative component.

Story ballets, of course, also portray characters and have a narrative. Traditional story ballets do not fall into this category, as they use the shapes of classical ballet costumes as their starting point, and details of character and story are added as a second step. Less traditional story ballets and other narrative dances count as theatrical if they base the design on its ability to convey the overall themes of the work and the character's personality. Works in this vein may range from translated traditional costumes to more realistic pedestrian clothing to theatrical.

Trey McIntyre—*The Vinegar Works* for Trey McIntyre Project (Premiere 2014)

Trey McIntyre conceived of a work comprised of vignettes from author Edward Gorey. For the resulting *Vinegar Works*, the costumes needed to function on several levels. They helped the dancers portray characters ranging from the Beastly Baby to Death himself. And McIntyre wanted the overall visual aesthetic to evoke the famous illustrations. The choreographer worked with costume designer Bruce Bui, and also with puppet and set designers Michael Curry and Dan Luce, to figure out what elements of the drawings were necessary to make their translation work. Evolving the final design took a lot of dialog back and forth. McIntyre recalls that "one idea was the costumes need to be 'drawn'—perhaps hand painted or with crosshatching—but ultimately that was not that interesting to either of us. Bruce came up with brilliant techniques to evoke [the look] with real texture and volume. He used light meshy fabrics in different tones of gray, ripping and stitching to suggest hatching." Bui echoed the Edwardian-era clothing of the book and its grayscale color palette. However, he not only had to recreate the aesthetics, he also had to make it danceable. He figured out how to give the costumes volume and shape without making them actually heavy so that the dancers wouldn't get too sweaty. Since the costumes sometimes changed the dancers' body shapes or affected their range of movement, McIntyre ensured that the costumes would be complete well ahead of time so that the dancers could rehearse in the actual garments.

McIntyre also enjoyed the creative problem-solving needed to incorporate puppets and masks into the dance. "My good friend Michael Curry, known for *The Lion King*, did the puppetry for the piece . . . The Death character is giant, as tall as the stage. The coat opens up and turns into a carousel. I loved talking— puppeteer and dancer together—to figure out the logic of how the pieces would work."

WEARABLE ART

While fashion designers and fine artists sometimes also do costumes for dance, this category is about the outcome, not the training of the designer. While clearly any dance costume can be considered a work of wearable art, this category is about sculptural forms created for the body: a costume not closely linked to a genre of clothing, something abstracted or heightened. While like any costume, this style should be compatible with the choreography, it also draws attention to itself as a piece of art. The cubist outfits designed by Pablo Picasso for the Ballet Russe's *Parade*, accented with jutting cones and flanked with layers of flat geometric shapes forming a wall above the dancer fall in this category. Wearable art might have the avant-garde beauty and abstraction of runway fashion or veer more towards performance art. Henrik Vibskov's suit covered with grass for Alexander Ekman's *Escapist* and cage-like body covering for *Swan Lake* accommodate the dance but also suggest art gallery installations.

Jenny Rocha—*Battledress* for Rocha Dance Theater (Premiere 2013)

Jenny Rocha is a choreographer who also creates her own costume designs. For *Half Heard* (2019 premiere) one of her constructions was a wide-brimmed hat that supported a curtain of fringe, forming a cylinder that completely hid the dancer. She had a second layer of fringe suspended from her shoulders. "I had [the dancer] shake a lot so it actually looked like she was fearful . . . Her leg will come out and it will look very sensual but then she hides it back underneath. There is also a sensuality with that costume." For Rocha's earlier *Battledress*, she wanted to create a work about armor, but tied to female stereotypes like the housewife. For one of the dancers, she sought to create a costume "like a jewel box ballerina but sort of abstract. So, I made a red rose cage that resembles a tutu." She then accented the costume with gloves edged with large spikes. The dancers wore jeweled face cages reminiscent of fencing masks, topped with sculptural headpieces. Some of the headpieces evoked oversized tufts of barbed wire, spikes out in all directions and another was formed of tubular hair rollers stacked into a pyramid.

Rocha's own experience living in New York City inspired *Battledress*. She wanted to be strong and confident, but also find a way to be vulnerable, to let down the armor in order to be an artist. "I wanted the armor to be protective, and also strength, but also something to hide behind when I needed to . . . What happens to me when I take off the armor? What is that vulnerable self when I take it off? How did the armor affect me?" Over the course of the piece, the dancers take off the bejeweled armor but also put it back on. As they rehearsed, they realized that they felt exposed when they took off the layers of protection, but in exposing themselves, "showing you who I am makes us feel powerful."

BODY MODIFICATIONS AND TRANSFORMATIONS

Dancers have used costumes that hide, amplify or completely transform the shape of the body from the earliest days. In concert dance, iconic examples of this form include Loie Fuller's 1891 *Serpentine Dance*, a flowing manipulation of giant silk skirts, and Martha Graham's 1930 work *Lamentation*, where the dancer created sculptural forms inside a tube of stretch fabric.

Elena Comendador—*The Calling* by Jessica Lang (Premiere 2005)

Choreographer Jessica Lang's piece *The Calling*, featured a dancer who wore a giant skirt that covered the stage. Costume designer Elena Comendador recalled that the skirt, made of 20-foot long gores or segments, travelled in its own suitcase. Lang revisited the work in several versions with different dancers. Comendador noted that the tone of the piece changed depending on the casting, and the version performed by a man "looked more preacher-like." For the original version, the designer watched the dancer and choreographer rehearse in the soft jersey garment, which "stretches and drapes wonderfully." They "had to figure out how to walk in it. [The dancer] had to slide and not pick up her feet so as not to step on it. It changed the whole movement style and added to the feel of the piece." Lang conceived of the idea for the skirt, and Comendador collaborated with her on shape and scale as she constructed it. To balance out the skirt, Lang asked her to design a top that would not appear solid. And so, the designer developed a skin tone leotard "with lace appliques to be like a tree."

Ingri Fiksdal—*Hoods* (Premiere 2014)

For one work, the costume created a transformation of not only the bodies of the dancers, but also of the entire performance space and the audience's perceptions. Choreographer Ingri Fiksdal created *Hoods* for which the costumes were "kind of the main operating principle." Costume designers Signe Becker and Anette Nan Lindrupsen created similar costumes for the performers, the audience and also for ten human-sized puppets. The loose robe-like outfits were accompanied by hats and veils that covered the face. As the audience arrived, they were given costumes and then let into the space five at a time. While their faces were masked and the space was dimly lit, they could see that others were in the room already. However, they didn't know who was there to perform and who to observe, or even who was human. With the work, Fiksdal sought to blur the lines of a conventional performance venue so that "everyone is sharing the same space." She wanted to "investigate the relationship between scenography and costume, choreography and performers. And, to see if we can create . . . maybe not equality, but that they are all playing [a variety of] important roles within the whole. The addition of the puppets added a facet to explore—the human/non-human binary."

When the audience was given their costumes, they were told that they were free to roam the space, or to sit or stand still. The dancers followed an improvisational structure, doing tasks that the choreographer set up for them, but Fiksdal also left spaces open for the unexpected to happen. "It was difficult to figure out how much to do," she recalled. "If it's too set, it's just like any choreography that you watch, in a sense. But if we did too little and the audience did nothing, then it ends up being nothing. Some performances worked better than others." The audience's reactions to the piece ranged from wanting to become performers to hanging back around the periphery. Some swung puppets that were suspended from the ceiling or rolled with them on the floor. Some moved tentatively across the space, feeling liberated by their anonymity. Other people stood safely by the wall, becoming part of the scenery.

COMPLETELY UNIQUE

Sometimes people want something strikingly unusual. Costume designers, for dance and other media, often roll their eyes when they are asked for something never before seen. They know that there is not really any such thing, and sometimes such a request feels ignorant or impossible. And yet, while on the one hand nothing can be created out of nowhere, every artist's creation is also uniquely their own. Every artist is a product of their past and present experiences.

We are all influenced by our predecessors and by the world around us. No costume design ideas, in dance or otherwise, can truly be out of nowhere. Even designs for science fiction and fantasy reference and combine influences from the animal world, other cultures and past time periods. *Star Wars* costumes blend medieval and Japanese shapes, *Black Panther* mixes elements from traditional African cultures with Western futuristic aesthetics. Ancient patterns, silhouettes and embellishments meld with sleek modern superhero armor. Although no costume is a whole new genre, looks can be combined in new and ingenious ways. The novelty of the costume can be bold, drawing attention to its innovation, or it can be so subtle that the audience ignores the costume's origins completely.

NOTES

1 Patricia Leigh Beaman, *World Dance Cultures: from Ritual to Spectacle* (New York: Routledge, 2018), section 1.2.

2 "Indian Classical Dances," Cultural India, accessed May 15, 2020, www.culturalindia.net/indian-dance/classical/index.html

3 "Damba as a Festival and Dance Form," Arts Ghana, July 11, 2014, http://artsghana.org/damba-as-a-festival-and-dance-form/

4 Takiyah Nur Amin, "The African Origins of an American Art Form," in *Jazz Dance: A History of the Roots and Branches*, ed. Lindsay Guarino and Wendy Oliver (Gainesville: University Press of Florida, 2014), 38–39.

5 "How the Four Temperaments Used to Dress," The Australian Ballet, May 28, 2013, https://australianballet.com.au/behind-ballet/how-the-four-temperaments-used-to-dress

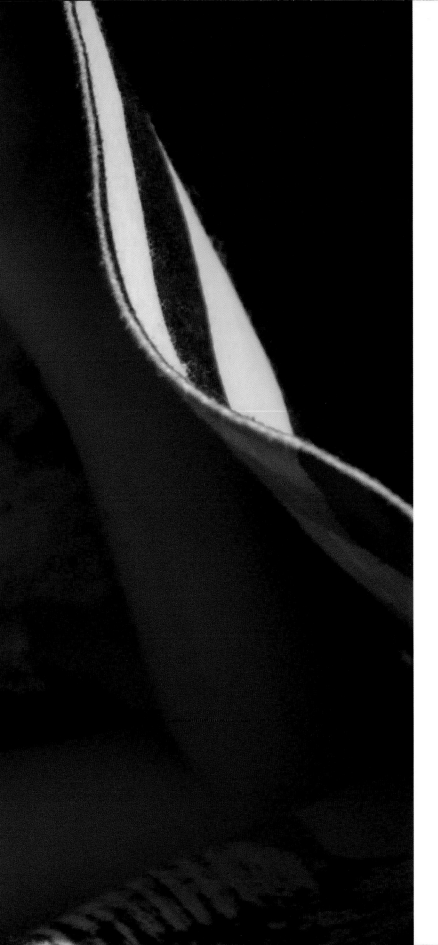

Case Study #3
STATE

CHOREOGRAPHER—INGRI FIKSDAL

CO-DIRECTOR/DRAMATURG—JONAS CORELL PETERSEN

PREMIERE DATE—2016

DATE PHOTOGRAPHED—FEBRUARY 2019

PERFORMANCE VENUE—THE CONTEMPORARY ARTS CENTER IN CINCINNATI

MUSIC—LASSE MARHAUG

COSTUME DESIGN—HENRIK VIBSKOV

LIGHTING DESIGN—ØYVIND WANGENSTEEN AND PHILLIP ISAKSEN

A close-up of one of the printed hoods designed by Henrik Vibskov

Dancers as boulder-like forms at the start of the piece

Rannei Grenne in one of the printed capes

The audience sits in curved rows of seats that encircle the performance space. As they settle in, some of the stage crew serve them small shots of Norwegian liquor as a welcome, while the dancers casually wander through the space, warming up. Then the lights shift, low thrumming music starts and bolder-like forms appear on the floor. The dancers, completely covered in pale green fabric, slowly shift position. The shapes under the fabric are barely discernable as human bodies so it's hard to recognize if the protrusions are leg, arm or head. Each dancer is isolated in their own section of the stage; their movement is separate but related. They evoke glaciers, or possibly embryos. After quite a while, the pace picks up and the dancers, now standing, begin to thrash—they sway and bend violently in time to drumbeats. Later they begin to spin through the space. A costumed member of the crew periodically circles the stage, spraying haze from a hand-held machine.

Ingri Fiksdal is a Norwegian choreographer who researches affective choreography. She studies the results of experiencing a dance on the performers and also on the audience in terms of their perception, the emotions they feel, and the actual physical experience as well. She seeks to develop choreographic methods that help her to explore the affective potential of dance. *STATE* is based on a study of ritual dance from a wide range of cultures and time periods, and seeks to create an immersive performance of dance, costume, light and sound that can affect the mental and bodily state of both the audience and the performers.

The dancers remove the capes, revealing tan unitards decorated with a snake-like print in vivid aqua and red. In view of the audience they don large sculptural pleated skirts, which had previously been standing by themselves like a row of oversized lanterns at the edge of the dancefloor. The skirts echo the aqua and red of the unitards, although the design is splintered into shards interspersed with other graphic patterns that simultaneously contrast and balance. The dancers unhook a few of the large pleats and manipulate the heavy fabric around their shoulders and then scoop it over their heads, abstracting their forms even further. Later they hold part of the skirt overhead as they turn, creating spiraling kaleidoscopes of dots and stripes. The built-up energy gradually releases along with the skirts themselves. The dancers slowly shed them using careful footwork. They sway from side to side, and as their arms gracefully gesture up and out, they subtly step on the skirts, causing the pleats to detach one by one from the waistband, until the skirts eventually pile up, nest-like, on the floor.

The five dancers come together into groupings as the piece progresses, but no one touches until around halfway through. At times they appear quite human, and tenderly entwine arms or lift each other into different formations. At other times they wear sheer mesh face-coverings printed with the same snake-like graphic as the unitards. The hoods de-emphasize their humanity and make them seem more primal or symbolic. The human form is altered again when they put on the capes from the first section and manipulate the fabric like acrobats spinning plates. Eventually, the dancers flip their capes over one by one, and the whirling circles change from the light green face to a bold geometric dark brown print. The dancers themselves nearly disappear in the swirling fabric and the shadowy lighting.

Fiksdal developed the piece in collaboration with her husband Jonas Corell Petersen, a theater director. Although married, this was only their second time collaborating. They created the concept for *STATE* together and Petersen served as the dramaturg. They sought to examine the overall idea of ritual dance by making a wide-ranging study of dances from all continents, from both the past and present. They looked for links between very disparate cultures. Petersen explained that "you can see the emerging dances of different cultures, but also the perspective of blurred borders, cultures crossing states." For example, when they examined a meditational dance from Bhutan called *cham*, they realized that certain elements when put into slow motion start to look like classical ballet. They also saw trends based on human anatomy. "The body of a human is limited in the sense that it cannot do any type of movement, so then across cultures and across time it can look the same." Fiksdal chose the title *STATE* because of the overlapping multiple meanings the term could have: mental state, state of being, as a verb (to state) and also nation state. Through the study of different cultures, she sought to find connections that span time and place, and the nation state becomes all one. "There are commonalities such as the spinning movement, different types of drumbeats, and repetition that you can find across all continents."

Fiksdal explained that in *STATE* some of the source material is more recognizable, while other cultural dances were just used by the dancers as a starting point to build new material through improvisation, based on a reaction to certain qualities they observed. An Ethiopian ritual dance called *Zār* is one of the styles Fiksdal found inspiring. "It has had so many different versions, the meaning has changed through thousands of years of the culture. For us that was

Louis Schou-Hansen manipulates his cape in fog

A dancer is silhouetted in her mesh hood

The cast adds red socks for one more mechanized section. The felt skirts stand like scenery in the background

of specific interest, as it shows how ritual changes over time. It's not a static thing—it's something that drives culture. As well as being driven by culture." Petersen spoke about their desire to investigate modern rituals that were not church, wedding ceremonies or funerals. He had "an interest in finding out how rituals work today, and what is the connection, if any, between state and ritual." Petersen and Fiksdal were able to conduct research during a residency in Montreal. They traveled to different Pow Wows of the First Nations to observe. They sought to understand the function of the Pow Wow in older times and in the present, and the ways in which the meetings built and strengthened the community. They learned that the gatherings were as vital now as when they originated, even if the specifics of the event and its purpose had evolved.

With *STATE*, Fiksdal and Petersen strove to create more of an immersive, ritual-like experience, rather than a standard concert dance performance. The audience is served small shots of alcohol at the beginning and again in the middle. The entire piece has the immediacy of a spontaneous event. The "music is performed live; the lights are not programmed—he [the board operator] controls it manually. They adjust to the space and play or perform together, the lights and the music." The music is often very rhythmic and repetitive, and at times is designed to be not only heard but felt by the audience as certain frequencies vibrate through the floor. The choice to perform the piece in the round breaks down borders between performers and audience. During much of the performance, the audience sees their peers opposite quite clearly, although at other times, with use of haze and lighting, they are obscured. The staging of the work also blurs the barrier between audience and performers. The musicians and light board operator are in full view and wear similar costumes to the dancers. When the dancers rest between sections or change costume pieces, they do not leave the playing area. Petersen states that "having these kinds of pauses or open changes of costume [create transparency]—now we change into something different. Not to create one coherent character or one coherent ritual but to have many different ones. Allowing the performers and the audience to step out of what had been."

Just after the audience is served a second round of drinks, Fiksdal and Petersen switch gears on purpose, partly, as Fiksdal joked, "to wake people up." This section of the dance was conceived very purposely as a break, and the dancers change to a more mechanized quality of movement. They all put on bright red socks, and perform quick, precise, angular movements exactly timed to the insistent beat of the music. The dancers' arms are held like the hands of

a clock, moving in sync or in precise counterpoint. Fiksdal saw the movement as evoking rituals like military parades, or even the Olympic Games opening ceremony in China. Petersen pointed out that this section was purposely "a very different quality than the rest—very hard or 'anti-soft' . . . musically it stands out being very rhythmical and keeps the same beat the whole time."

Fiksdal developed a particular interest in trance rituals and whether a dance in this genre could produce a specific mental state in the audience. She created the opening section, the iceberg-like shapes which she calls "Mountain," not to evoke ritual but instead, to ease the audience into the experience, "to empty out expectation . . . By starting in this very slow manner, we would like to tune the audience into watching in this slow pace." She sought to minimize the standard dance audience's "expectation of wanting things to happen, wanting to be impressed." While the choreography is often quite obviously difficult, and the dancers show virtuosity of balance, endurance and technique, Petersen said that with *STATE* they also wanted to "take the focus away from the individual performance of the dancers. Hopefully you forget which dancer is where." The work ends with the dancers spinning in their graphic capes, as the music builds in a gradual crescendo. The theater becomes nearly opaque with haze, pierced with blinking light. The audience is completely immersed in the powerful thumping bass notes. Watching the spinning dark and light patterns on the capes, they feel nearly hypnotized by the chaotic atmosphere. Then, the atmosphere gradually releases, the dancers slow, the music fades, and the audience is drawn slowly back to themselves.

As they created the piece, Fiksdal and Petersen would discuss ideas in development at home. She worked with the dancers in rehearsal, and then once or twice a week he would come by and give feedback. While she was the choreographer, he contributed not only to the dramaturgy, the ideas behind the work, but also to the overall structure of the choreography and the performance. Other collaborators were also essential to developing the piece. They commissioned music from Lasse Marhaug and enlisted lighting designers Øyvind Wangensteen and Phillip Isaksen. Fiksdal and Petersen had not previously collaborated with Henrik Vibskov, but they knew his work by reputation and contacted him to see if he would design costumes for *STATE*.

Vibskov is a well-known Danish fashion designer. He also designs installations for art museums and galleries, as well as costumes and scenery for theater, opera and dance. Fiksdal and Petersen were interested in working with Vibskov not only for his bold and playful

Dancers in the heavy pleated felt skirts and mesh hoods

Dancer Nuria Guiu Sagarra

Schou-Hansen in a
fringed hat

aesthetic, but also because he has a large fabrication studio at his disposal. Since the costumes had to withstand months of rehearsal in addition to the wear and tear of actual performance, they sought someone with the resources to have things constructed that would endure. Vibskov's main business is fashion. Between his studio in Denmark and a shop in New York, he employs over 50 people including architects, graphic designers, patternmakers and stitchers. He explains with a laugh "We couldn't be 50 people if we were just doing costume, we would be . . . one." He likes doing a variety of stage work, including theater, but he feels most drawn to dance since he danced in his youth, and also because he has performed professionally on drums throughout his life. He works simultaneously in different genres and thrives on the cross-pollination that often happens between his various projects. "It's nice when we are busy . . . a little bit chaotic even . . . Maybe some of the dance costumes go into the catwalk, or vice versa."

Fiksdal contacted Vibskov, explained the concept of the piece, and sent him numerous images of different ritual dances from their research. Once he accepted, Fiksdal, Petersen and Vibskov had several meetings to discuss the ideas in more depth, but overall the costume designer had nearly free rein. This style of costume collaboration was new for all of them. Both designer and choreographer more typically develop the costumes in tandem with the choreography, not before. For *STATE*, the costumes were not only designed but built before any of the rehearsals started, and the garments were used to generate a lot of the choreographic ideas. Fiksdal didn't suggest any costume shapes to the designer or describe the specific choreographic movements she envisioned. Vibskov said "As I remember we talked not so much about this piece, but about things that could have a transformation, could be used in different ways." Fiksdal stated that she also sought "something that would have dramaturgy or development within the costume that you could see somehow. But then we didn't say anything more. It was him that came up with the skirts, the capes." They had seen head coverings in some of the designer's previous work and suggested that they would like an element of the costumes to be in that vein.

Their initial discussions were fairly brief, and then Vibskov went to work. In addition to the images of ritual dance, the other starting point he had was the music. The designer recalled that "we talked about the music, [that it would be] darker, more drone-like, more noise. It was done by this classic black metal artist Lasse Marhaug, now a noise musician." He had not previously worked on a dance where the costumes took the lead, rather than following the choreography. "The way we did this is very opposite of normal. It was really nice, actually, from our side . . . it was really freeing."

He brainstormed with his studio, and developed shapes first, and then prints and surface designs. "We worked on the folded massive pleated skirt that could be connected, [fastening] all the skirts into one big skirt." Vibskov is a fashion designer and costume designer, but his first love is music. He started in music before he studied visual art, and still performs as a drummer. Since the music for *STATE* had not yet been composed, he listened to the composer's previous works to find inspiration for the prints. He describes how he literally sees color in music. As he listened to Marhaug's work, he was certain that bold colors were called for. He did not want a black and white scheme. The compositions also gave him his inspiration for the graphics. He felt a "dusty paintbrush effect." The designs for the fabric were digitally printed, which his studio does in-house. Some of the graphics came from images he was already using for his fashion line but scaled up to the maximum.

To facilitate the kinds of use the costumes needed, he paid special attention to the materials. He made large capes with a double-sided fabric. One side was a pale mint green, the other a bold dark brown and white print. He had to find something with the right body to keep its shape, move with the right kind of flow, and thick enough that the dark print did not show through to the pastel green side. For the heavy pleated skirts, he found a material that was "more like a felt carpet, not something you normally use in a costume." He liked how the material could hold the pleats, be flexible, and also was made of the right kind of synthetic fibers to print on. In fact, he was so happy with this unusual material, which has held up well for three years and does not wrinkle, that he has been trying to find it again for use in other projects.

Vibskov recalled that the actual design process was quite rapid. Fiksdal seemed to like his initial suggestions, "had few comments and then we did it." He also was on a tight timeline to fit the construction into his studio between other projects. Most of the costumes did not need to be precisely fit to the dancers—pleated skirts, circular capes and stretchy bag-like hoods. An employee from his studio travelled to fit the base unitards on the dancers but Vibskov himself did not see the costumes in use until the premiere. Once the costumes were in rehearsal, Fiksdal and her dancers improvised with them. Petersen stated that "it's also a new way of working for both of us, letting the costumes dictate the dramaturgy." They developed a great deal of material, but Fiksdal culled the ideas. She found it "a challenge, because Heinrik is such a renowned fashion

designer. We wanted to be sure [the piece] doesn't just become a display for these amazing costumes. We wound up cutting a lot of very beautiful stuff because it becomes *too* beautiful. There has to be a balance for the piece to work as a whole . . . we didn't want it to become only about what the costumes could do."

Vibskov was pleased when he finally saw the work. "I went to the premiere, which was inside a mountain in Austria, in a cave. That was the first time I actually saw the . . . full costumes. I thought it was *wild*. The music was so loud. But in a good way . . . The music inside the cave was just at the limit of . . . torture."

3

Styles of Collaboration

Any working relationship functions better if everyone knows what the expectations of their role are. While every artist has their own preferred mode of working and collaborating, methods of planning design for dance can be divided into different categories. For discussion purposes these are set as discrete examples, but there is in practice a continuum between the various styles, and many processes may fall between two of them. Or choreographers may work in one style for costume and another for lighting or another design area. Many artists modify their working style with different collaborators, and also depending on the subject or style of the piece. Examining different methods may inspire practitioners to try a new approach.

CHOREOGRAPHER AS MAIN DRIVER

Unlike most theater and film directors, who work from a preexisting script or text, a choreographer of a new piece is not only staging a work but creating it from scratch. They often envision not just the choreographic steps, but other visual and sonic aspects of the work that are intrinsic to their piece. They see what the dancers' bodies look like; not only the movement but also the color and shapes that enhance or hide them. They imagine the performance space is there a brightly lit cyc or is the backdrop for the dancers a brick wall covered in graffiti? They decide how a work begins, which might involve how the dancers enter from the wings, or a gradual fade up first of dissonant noise, and then of a spotlight revealing bodies on the floor. The level of control a choreographer exerts can range in intensity from the choreographer functioning as an "auteur," having

dancers from Contra-Tiempo perform *joyUS justUS* (see Case Study #1)

a total vision of the piece, to a softer influence where they specify guiding principles and ideas for the team to refine as they create designs or compose.

This style does not mean that the choreographer does all the decision-making, but that their conceptualization of the piece is not just about the initial themes and the steps of the dance, or even the story they seek to tell, but about the wider look and feel of the work. Choreographers are usually very visual people, and their conception of a dance may include thinking how a dancer moves in and out of a pool of light, a specific pair of flowing pants, or a reflective, metallic color palette. Some commission music for their piece, so as not to be constrained by the shape, length and tempo of a preexisting piece.

While the level of detail in the choreographer's instructions may vary, the designer's job is to work within a set framework. The choreographer establishes the overall idea for the piece. They set the theme, establish a structure, choose the music. The costume designer may start work before or after the actual choreography has been created, but either way their mission is to develop the choreographer's ideas into workable costumes. The costume idea the choreographer presents may be quite detailed: "a purple dress with a long, flared skirt with a slit and a bodice with nude mesh panels." But the costume designer still figures out the details of the bodice, the shade of purple, the best placement for the slit, and the style of the straps. Or the instructions could be as general as "a selection of street clothing so that the dancers seem like store window mannequins." Then it is up to the designer to figure out a grouping of five outfits that will communicate "mannequin" or "store window" to the audience, choose a color palette, and make sure that the clothes will accommodate the dancers' movement needs. Whether broad or specific, designers do tend to prefer that a choreographer give them parameters within which they can work, rather than just telling them what the design should be.

Trey McIntyre and Reid & Harriet Design—*Big Ones* for BalletX (Premiere 2016)

When Trey McIntyre stated his costume idea for his piece entitled *Big Ones*, set to the music of Amy Winehouse, Reid Bartelme explained that he and his co-designer, Harriet Jung, took the idea to make the dancers into superhero chocolate bunnies in stride. "We didn't ask why. The idea seemed really fun. It seemed like something that would be exciting for us to figure out. We work with a couple of people like that. We like what is going on in their head, so we are happy to execute that vision."

Trey McIntyre had been thinking about making a piece based on the music of Amy Winehouse for a while, but he wanted to be sure he had something to say about her music so he would not just be illustrating it. For the choreographer to begin his process, he needed to find a personal connection to her and her songs. When watching a documentary about her life, "one of the things that struck me—and this is all my projection—what I imagine was that part of her downfall was how exceptional she was. She was in a world around people who were regular people and she was this shining star," McIntyre explained. In his view, while people want to be exceptional to be admired and loved, being exceptional is also to be set apart and lonely.

McIntyre approaches each dance he creates as a set of puzzles to figure out. One of the puzzles for *Big Ones* was the costumes—both what they should look like and how they would function. He wanted the costumes for the dance to make the dancers unique and exceptional. As he spent time ruminating on the themes for this work, things he encountered over the course of his day sparked his imagination. At a friend's house, he saw a wine rack that looked like antlers, and holding it to his head, he liked the encumbrance it provided. While the final idea did evoke rabbits, in fact chocolate rabbits, he explained that the idea developed from antlers or ears into wanting something that would relate to the human body.

As he and the designers worked on creating a dramatic headpiece for the dancers to wear, he began to see the ear-like shape protruding overhead as an extension of the spine, and also as something that mirrored the shape of legs. The design for the headpieces needed to synthesize several ideas. In addition to creating an interesting aesthetic shape, he also wanted the dancers to be a bit ridiculous. "Amy Winehouse was this tiny person with hair as tall as she was, with no apologies." The costume that covers the torso of the dancers also translated the idea of being exceptional, by making the dancers seem like superheroes. McIntyre wanted to combine these influences in a way that would somehow also allow the audience to take the piece and the dancers seriously. He sought a "very specific balance of fun, humor, sexuality, playfulness but not laughing at those costumes or making fun of them."

When he met with the designers, Bartelme and Jung, he gave them "stacks" of research images of superheroes showing the aesthetic he was drawn to, and he also gave them a specific idea of the ear-like headpieces he had in mind. For a color he wanted something deep and sensual, and the shine of chocolate as well as the color inspired the fabric choice. The costume designers found a rich brown stretch fabric with a leather-like sheen that they could tailor into short, sleeveless unitards that give a solid, broad-shouldered effect to the eight dancers, and highlight their athletic physiques. They developed the idea to add mesh panels to give the looks detail, as well as to provide additional stretch and help with movement. The men had a sheer band at the ribcage and the women just below the waist, and both had triangular insets over the shoulders that hug the musculature and added a dynamic diagonal to the look.

The trick in designing the hats was to evoke rabbit ears without being too specific. Making the hats light and strong and keeping the nearly two-foot-high ears in place during an active dance proved a technical challenge. Although not trained in hat-making, Bartelme and Jung learned to work with Fosshape, a felt-like thermoplastic material, and molded the ears over clay forms that they also sculpted. They found a graceful shape that sprouted from the back of the head and curved forward as it extended up. The curve gave a nice sleek appearance, and also kept the weight centered over the dancer's body. The base of each ear formed a full tube that tapered quickly into a half-pipe. The cylindrical shape helped stabilize the form, supplemented by boning, and the hollowness gave a bit more riff on the chocolate bunny allusion.

Ray Mercer and Elena Comendador—*This I Know for Sure* for Dayton Contemporary Dance Company (Premiere 2017)

This I Know for Sure was the second piece Ray Mercer choreographed for Dayton Contemporary Dance Company. He considers himself a very physical choreographer, focused on technique and line. The title is an indirect reference to Mercer's approach to dance. "As a choreographer, I wanted to confirm where I was, my choreographic voice . . . there are certain elements about my choreography that I know for sure." The work has six sections, vignettes on a variety of themes, such as social issues and relationships. One of Mercer's favorite sections is a trio of women. "I've always felt that women are the strongest people on the face of this earth, and I wanted to celebrate that. They all look very different, and their approach to dance is very different."

Mercer had already created the piece and presented it at a workshop before costume designer Elena Comendador joined the project. But the two had collaborated before, so they were able to navigate a more compressed design process. Mercer felt confident that "she knows my sensibility." He values Comendador's ability to "create small details that pop onstage" and that as a former dancer, "she knows a dancer's body." They had an initial meeting after Comendador saw the dancers run the work. He explained his ideas: simple vest-like tunics with shorts to show the leg, and tailcoats for a later section of the piece. For Mercer, the coats "represented power and structure. How we can put it on, and it gives us power. We take it off and it is stripped away." Mercer was thinking of the board room—gray suits with a hint of color like a tie.

Comendador took notes and then a week later came back with sketches and color ideas. She knew that Mercer liked simplicity, and "he always wants them to be people, [but] . . . an abstract version of people." Additionally, his dances are far too physical for "real clothes literally . . . He likes gray—every choreographer likes gray—it lights well and it's not an emotional color, non-committal. Not passionate, just dark and mysterious." She took Mercer's suggestion of a color accent but translated it into an applique used decoratively on the tunic, a slash of dark red, rather than the tie or scarf he first imagined. She was afraid that a full jacket would not work with the movement, so she made the tailcoats without sleeves. Mercer approved her designs. "I fell in love with the initial sketch."

The dancers wore black bike shorts and the women had black sports bras. For the first section, they wore the tailored gray vest-like tunics, each with slightly different detailing. The tunics are slim but have slits at the bottom to give a sense of movement when the dancers turn. For a middle section, the dancers removed the tunics, and exposed more skin in just the black shorts for the men, and shorts and bras for the women. Later, they added the tailcoats. Comendador understood that the dancers needed socks for the choreography, to be able to slide, but she commented, "I hate socks because it really does cut the line of the leg." She tried to suggest flesh tone socks or ballet shoes, "but it's such a trend right now that I just go with it.

[And, I realized that] skin-tone socks looked odd. Dark socks bring out a harder look."

Mercer was pleased with the product. "When I saw the costumes on the dancers, it was exactly what I had envisioned."

GROUP/TEAM EVOLUTION

The next style of collaboration is one where the choreographer is still the leader of the process but does not give the collaborators specific ideas for the visuals of the design. Instead, the choreographer has a road map for where the piece should go and how it should get there, but the design evolves alongside the choreography. This is not to say that designs for the "choreographer main driver" style do not also evolve as needed during the rehearsal process. But, in this style, the goal from the outset is to evolve the

Dayton Contemporary Dance Company dancers Countess V. Winfrey and Michael Green perform *This I Know for Sure* by Ray Mercer with costume design by Elena Comendador.

dancers Elizabeth Ramsey, Winfrey and Nile Alicia Ruff in Comendador's red-accented vest tops

dancer Stevie Lamblin is held by two other dancers

ideas together, and the designer is more embedded in the overall conceptualization process.

Most creative teams working in this style begin either by having discussions with the whole group, or each designer separately with the choreographer. The choreographer will share ideas of theme, movement style, structure and any other factors that inspired the inception of the piece. Designers ask questions about mood, music, source material, logistics such as physicality or partnering, as well as any physical factors like the performance space, use of projections, etc. These conversations, and certainly responding to the music if there is prechosen music, will give the designers an initial spark. However, whether finished choreography or movement phrases in development, designers need to see the dancers' bodies, motions and groupings in space to figure out a design. The abstraction of dance movement can never be adequately captured in conversation. Designers need to observe not only the types of movement, but how the dancers interpret the movement. Seeing the rehearsal (or a video of it if logistics demand) lets the designer respond to the gesture, emotional quality and how the dancers fill the space. The designer can respond directly to the movement they observe and also have their own emotional or intuitive reaction.

Depending on the designer, inspiration for a costume design might be triggered by seeing colors when listening to the music, thinking of an exotic bird as the choreographer describes an influential poem, or imagining a type of fabric moving on the dancers' bodies. Once they have some concrete ideas, they share research images and/or sketches with the choreographer to determine if they are headed in the right direction. The designer adapts the costume ideas based on feedback from the choreographer and imagery from the other collaborators on the project. They also continue to deepen their own connection to the piece by watching more rehearsal, doing further research, and sketching. They may hone the ideas further by developing and testing prototypes. Many choreographers feel that they can't fully complete their work without knowing what the dancers will actually look like. What parts of the body will be seen or hidden? How will the fabric move? What kind of stage picture will the groupings of colors create? Certainly, especially for any unusual shapes or materials, working with and testing prototypes early on is vital for all involved. The choreographer may make subtle or even significant adjustments to the choreography, or even to the overall conceptualization of the piece, based on the costume design ideas.

This category also includes devised pieces, where the choreographer leads the piece, but the dancers assist in creating the choreography.

At the outset of the creation process, the final product is not yet clearly envisioned, so the overall piece evolves as it comes into focus. Designers for devised pieces must be in constant communication with their collaborators during the rehearsal process. Additionally, they have to balance waiting for the dance to take enough shape that they can design costumes that work with the movement and the content of the dance with having enough time to actually execute the designs.

E. Shura Pollatsek and Christopher K. Morgan—*Halcyon* for Christopher K. Morgan & Artists (Premiere 2013)

Christopher K. Morgan uses his choreography to process experiences and emotions in his own life, or ideas that he wants to explore. *Halcyon* was prompted by thoughts about his own maturing, and reflections on past memories. "It's about memory and how it shifts in the passage of time. When I came back to things, I noticed that some of my memories were looking more glowing and beautiful than the reality was when I was experiencing them," the choreographer recalled. One of the phrases he used during our initial design meeting was "the color of memory." As a designer, I found this phrase very evocative and noted it as something to explore. Morgan and I also discussed how memories can fade in and out, which gave another visual cue I could develop. Morgan did not have any set plan for the costumes, other than that he wanted the dancers to be in clothing-based shapes, with skirts for the women and pants for the men, but something abstracted not pedestrian.

Morgan commissioned a sculptor, Bryan Sullivan, who made transparent life casts of each performer in packing tape, which he arranged around the stage like ghostly after-images of the dancers. The work had an overall ethereal quality to it, which drew me to a cool color scheme. I chose light gray for the base of the costumes and a different accent color for each dancer, ranging from teal to blue to purple.

I first worked on the idea of memories fading in and out. I thought of partially developed photos and eroding old murals. This led me to wanting the costumes to have some sections fully colored and other parts left plain, as if the paint had worn off. I kept the clothing shapes simple and chose a matte jersey that would show the lines of the body with its drape, without being tight-fitting. Morgan and I had our next meeting, and he liked the direction I was heading. I showed him rough pencil sketches of clothing shapes, shaded in different directions for each dancer. One had the shoulder colored in and then faded out diagonally across the chest, another was boldest at the waist and faded upwards. I showed him color samples, and we discussed which hues would look best for each of the five dancers, especially as they partnered. When I watched the choreography in rehearsal, I noticed a lot of spiraling movements. I designed insets of sheer mesh, a corkscrew around one pant leg and a spiral on one side of the skirts, which added to the eroding feeling.

The final look for the costumes was a sleeveless top with an asymmetrical neckline, the same for each dancer. Around the midsection, each had a wide sash that gradually narrowed as it wrapped multiple times around the waist, like a crescent roll or another type of spiral. The triangle shifted color from pale to dark, so each layer contrasted with the one behind it. The men's pants were loose enough to have some movement and the women had flaring skirts. I created the eroding color by painting each dancer's costume with noticeable brush strokes, preserving the rough feeling from my pencil sketches. When we got to the theater, lighting designer Brian Allard added to the stage picture by using a lot of texture and strong diagonal beams of light through haze. His ethereal, desaturated lighting perfectly complemented the costumes and the sculptures.

Emily Morgan—*Realms of Amber* by Edgar Zendejas for Richmond Ballet (Premiere 2016)

Costume designer Emily Morgan described one of her all-time favorite collaborations at Richmond Ballet. In her initial conversation with choreographer Edgar Zendejas, he told her the dance originated from the idea that all souls have a feminine energy, which is the most positive side of humanity. The Mexican-born choreographer, who is known for choreographing both at dance companies like Hubbard Street Dance and for Cirque du Soleil, explained to her that in his culture the woman is the heart of the home—the emotional and spiritual center of the family. For this dance he juxtaposed the emotional strength of women against the physical strength of men. This idea led him to think of trees—the men as the solid trunks and the women as the stirring leaves. He chose to create the piece collaboratively with the company's dancers and designers. He gave each dancer a poem to interpret. And, he sent Morgan three photos of trees. Her only other starting point was the music, *Chants from the Valaam Monastery Choir*, by Russian Orthodox priests.

From these ingredients, she was able to explore freely where her imagination took her. "He was clear that he wanted the piece to not only be something of him, he wanted me to connect to it as well. It was a truly beautiful collaborative experience." Morgan described how while Zendejas was talking about the central role of women, her mind brought up an image of her grandmother's wedding dress

"which had a mock turtleneck illusion neckline and these covered buttons down the back. For me it felt like what I connect to, people with feminine energy have backbones of steel—soft on the outside, but incredibly strong inside. For me these covered buttons down their back became representative of a spine."

For color inspiration, Morgan drew on the tree imagery and thought about how just before a tree becomes barren in winter, it puts on a colorful show in autumn. She looked at images of trees and even collected leaves during her morning run to figure out which shades of red, purple and orange she wanted to use. The rich colors of the costumes, enhanced by the lighting design, brought this idea together.

Her grandmother's wedding dress inspired several other aspects of the design besides the buttons down the back: the overall bodice shape, sheer illusion sleeves and a band collar at the neck. When the designer saw the dancers in rehearsal, she knew she wanted a flowing silk skirt. However, finding an idea for the men didn't come to her as easily. As she looked for inspiration, she went back through the initial ingredients the choreographer had given her and dug into the music. While listening, she thought of how orthodox priests dress in a full-skirted cassock bound in by a wide belt, and from this developed her idea of very full-legged pants that look almost like a skirt, topped by a very wide waistband "almost like a corset." She left them bare-chested to accentuate their strength. To tie the look in with the women, she added in a sheer mesh panel at the front of each pant leg so that when they moved "you could see a flash of vulnerability."

The initial communication between designer and choreographer happened before Zendejas came to Richmond. They talked, and she sent him images. Once his residency began, she drew some initial sketches. She had to focus her ideas quickly, as the piece was developed during a two-week residency by the choreographer. Morgan likes to draw in the studio during rehearsal. As she watched the dancers' flowing, swirling movements, she began to see her design on their bodies. The choreographer gave her feedback on the shapes, what parts of the costume needed to be tight, which looser. However, it was the fabric samples that really helped him connect with her concept. She felt that it was seeing some larger pieces of the fabric and understanding not only the colors and textures but how it would move that really sold him on her design.

CHOREOGRAPHER AS DESIGNER

Any time clothing is chosen for a specific usage in a production, that means that costumes are designed. However, the person choosing may be someone without training in costume. In dance it is common for the choreographer to function as their own costume designer. This happens for a variety of reasons. Sometimes it is just a budgetary issue—many small companies cannot afford to employ a costume designer or a costume maker, so they pick out their own outfits from dancewear catalogs or shop from clothing stores. Many smaller and even some larger contemporary companies use designers for some pieces and go without when the vision is something that they feel they can implement on their own. Other times, the choreographer has such a specific vision that they don't feel the need to have a designer lend their expertise.

Most typically a choreographer functions as the designer when the costumes are simple, but sometimes the choreographer is also a visual artist, and creates more extensive or more specific designs that need to be custom-made. In this case, they often need expertise from a costume shop supervisor or costume director. Choreographers are not usually trained in costume construction, and so need a consultant who speaks the language of seams and draping to translate the design for the costume makers and ensure that the costume will function correctly for the movement of the dance. The consultant may help choose fabrics for stretch and launderability or give specifications on details like how neckline edges should be finished or what fastenings to use.

Kyle Abraham—*Pavement* for Abraham in Motion (Premiere 2012)

Kyle Abraham is an innovative choreographer who describes his style as "postmodern gumbo." The award-winning artist is very interested in working collaboratively. "I actually depend on my collaborators to give me thoughts or ideas on what to do or how they see the work. Then I can say 'no that's still not it', or 'yeah that's awesome'. And then it helps me to actually finish the dance." For most of his pieces, he includes the dancers in the choreography credit in the program. Abraham's choice of collaborators for design depends on the piece he is working on. While he always works with the same lighting designer, he has several costume designers on his short list. The content of the piece and the direction he envisions for the costumes determines which designer he contacts. One of his regular collaborators is his go-to for historically based works while he contacts the other for more abstract, gender-fluid pieces. However, there are also times that he prefers to serve as his own costume designer.

One such piece is *Pavement*. For works using contemporary-style clothing, he likes to put the outfits together himself. He fears that with a designer, the clothes "would be over-thought, and a little contrived. I can take more risks when I am personally shopping on my own time. I don't feel compelled to use any specific thing." *Pavement* was inspired by the 1991 film *Boyz n the Hood* but set in the historically Black neighborhoods Homewood and the Hill District of Abraham's native Pittsburgh. The piece is a fusion of street, contemporary, and ballet styles. The music ranges from Bach to Sam Cooke, accented with sirens, gun battles and snippets of dialog from the movie. The dancers, mainly Black men, but also one woman and two white men, represent the marginalized who grew up around a culture of violence. The choreography ranges from athletic and combative to lyrical to tender moments of embracing. Abraham wove in gestures from real life such as hands held behind as if in handcuffs but used as a motif, so they became part of the structure of the dance.

Since the piece was partially based on his own experiences growing up, he wanted to select clothes that captured that world for him. "I tried to create a nod to the early 90s but something that could also be seen as present day," Abraham explained. The dancers wore an assortment of loose pants and cargo shorts, with simple tanks and T-shirts. Everything looked natural and lived-in. Some wore plaid shirts open and others had them tied around the waist, which caused the loose fabric to stream behind them as they turned. While many of the clothes were drab, he also used a generous amount of color—pops of red, blue, turquoise and yellow. The dancers looked at home on the set, which was a wall of chain-link fencing accented with a basketball net. The dancers could move easily in these streetwear looks, but Abraham also made it part of the choreography that the dancers adjusted the clothes as needed, the way people do in real life. Each dancer had a different style of vintage sneakers, although in some sections they danced barefoot. The shoes were very important to Abraham—both the function and the appearance. Some of the choreography required not only sneakers, but ones that gave the right kind of flexibility and support. Dance sneakers did not look right, so he had to find actual vintage or vintage-looking shoes that supported the moves. He also used the shoes as an emblem—in a section of the dance they hung from a wire. Since the piece toured for four years, Abraham found himself continually shopping online for replacement shoes for different cast members.

Jenny Rocha—*Half Heard* for Rocha Dance Theater (Premiere 2019)

While Jenny Rocha also designs costumes for other choreographers, when she choreographs a dance, she always designs her own costumes. "I want to put my focus on dance and costume design and their fusion. I have always been visual." Rocha thinks of movement and costume together. She often comes up with an idea for a costume first, as she develops the initial themes of a work, and then the choreography follows. While she trained and began her performance career in modern and contemporary dance, she soon sought to branch out and "realized that I like being more of a hybrid dance artist. I like mixing different styles of dance, different audiences. I don't really like falling into just one category." Her explorations led her to an eight-year residency in Brooklyn, where she created The Painted Ladies, a troupe that she terms "neo burlesque." Being part of the nightlife genre influenced her work for Rocha Dance Theater, her concert dance company. "Everyone in nightlife does their own costume—it's part of their act."

Rocha learned to sew and make clothing from her mother, who owned a bridal shop and made custom dresses. Since she is self-taught as a designer, Rocha has created her own way to work through ideas. She rarely draws or creates visuals first. Instead "I see something in my head and then go shop." She finds elements that go well together, "different fragments." These may be fabrics, textures, or accessories. As she works with the materials and begins constructing the costumes, she refines her designs. When she designs for other choreographers, however, she does follow a more formal process, and has a dialog using found images and sketches before diving into shopping and sewing.

Rocha created *Half Heard* for Rocha Dance Theater to make "a parody of the macho construct. And how it's damaging for both male- and female-identifying people." The work is in two sections. The first has a more overt storyline, following a group of macho male businessmen as they are trained to be masculine, to be awful to women, to be aggressive. The second section is much more dream-like. The female characters from the first section "are spit out into this world of broken women. A surreal dreamy section where things do not always make sense. But you can see everyone's past on them, what they have been through." Despite the serious themes, "there is a lot of comedy in it. I wasn't sure how it would play, because it really isn't funny." However, her audience did laugh, and the uncomfortable laughter prompted them to question their own assumptions.

Rocha had the intent of women in drag playing the men from the outset. "I wanted to have people see what it would look like if we had female-identifying people on stage in that construct." The first choreography she created was a dance around a large table, and as she watched the dancers, she felt like they were in a boardroom. This initial impulse told her that businessmen were the type of male icon she wanted to portray, and so the costume for that section needed to be men's suits. The businessmen work through a "sort of boot camp" where they are trained to be masculine. Next, the choreography centers on a competition—the dancers vie for chairs. The men all get seats and the two female characters, wearing skirts, struggle for the remaining one.

For the second section of the work, Rocha created costumes that embodied different ways the women were "broken," each of which inspired its own movement quality. One dancer was completely covered in pink bows and tulle. "Her quality of movement is numb, slow, almost drunk. . . . Some movements are balletic too. The pretty ballerina does an awkward promenade and then falls to the floor, bouncing off the floor with all the tulle and the bows." Another dancer was in a pale blue ruffled dress, holding a bunch of blue balloons. "Some are inflated some are not. They float in mid-space sort of like her dreams. And she has long dark hair in front of her face— she is hiding behind her hair. It is clear through her movements that she is this deflated character." Another character was covered completely in fringe, and she shimmied a lot, as if quaking in fear.

Rocha also created two "warrior" characters who are strong and joyful. They had helmet-like headpieces boldly striped with bands of black and white rhinestones, topped with "these light pink flowers that are sort of mohawked down the center." They wore voluminous airy pale pink pants accented at the waist with black bow ties, topped with black mesh leotards. At the end of the piece, the dancers each lost an element—their headpieces, the balloons—accompanied by a soundscape of whispers. Rocha collected quotes of inappropriate comments women have endured in the workplace and layered them together. "It is not completely resolved, but these women have learned to let go of something that is holding them back and even the warriors are just their vulnerable selves at the end."

COSTUME-INSPIRED CHOREOGRAPHY

Many costume designers interviewed for this book dreamed of a project where they would design costumes and then choreography would be created from that. Many thought it would be novel to reverse the tables and have the limit be only their imagination. Some thought it would be interesting to give one costume to several choreographers and see what they each came up with. Some choreographers do in fact choose to create work from a costume. Typically in this case, however, the choreographer is the one who

dancers Green, Trezon Dancy and Quentin ApolloVaughn Sledge in *This I Know for Sure*

commissions the costume they want to work with—a skirt that fills the entire floor or a hoopskirt that hides a rolling chair—and then after the costume is designed and built, they create their choreography based on what the costume can do.

E. Shura Pollatsek—*Contratiempo* by Eric Rivera for WKU Dance Company (Premiere 2013)

Choreographers take inspiration from an infinite variety of things, and while not common, some do in fact start from an already designed costume or article of clothing. Choreographer Eric Rivera saw a strappy geometric leotard top in a clothing store. Envisioning it on a female dancer gave him the starting idea for his duet *Contratiempo*. The bold, graphic black stripes across the body moved him to choose music that was a duet between drums and guitar, and to create a duet where the woman was the guitar and the man the percussion. Luckily the piece that he purchased fit the dancer

he cast, and I worked with him as the costume designer to create a male costume with a similar look, and to adapt and strengthen the purchased leotard to function better on the woman's body for dancing. The slashes of black fabric across skin echoed the rhythms of the music as the dancers wrapped arms and legs around each other in a contemporary tango.

Jody Sperling and Mary Jo Mecca—*Ice Floe* for Time Lapse Dance (Premiere 2014)

Choreographer Jody Sperling of Time Lapse Dance works in the style of modern dance pioneer Loie Fuller. Fuller was known for creating dances based on manipulating a voluminous silk skirt or cape into swirling, abstract shapes. Sperling continues in this tradition, working with costume designers to create expansive extra-full circles of fabric that she and her company dancers manipulate with sticks that extend their arms. The costume must be fully created for

Matthew J. Talley in Matthew Evans' striking lighting

the piece to be choreographed. The fullness, weight and flow of the garment affect what the choreographer can create. (See more about Sperling in Case Study #5 later in this book.)

Sperling was one of several non-scientists selected as part of an outreach effort for an expedition to the Arctic in 2014 on a US Coast Guard polar icebreaker. The trip provided a chance for her to continue her investigation into dance based on physics and climate change. The landscape inspired the costume, and then the costume, plus the Arctic environment, dictated the choreography. Given her plan to actually dance on the pack ice, she knew that she would have to contend with cold and windy conditions. She and costume designer Mary Jo Mecca started with the practical decision that the costume needed to be a heavier silk and less voluminous than her other costumes. Sperling usually works with a closed garment, like a dress or poncho, but they decided to do a cape with an open front. She wore it over a white unitard that gave some insulation against the cold. Sperling recalled that "Mary Jo says she likes when

something loose is paired with something that's tight—it creates a nice contrast." The look was finished with sturdy lace-up boots, also in white, and a headband to insulate her ears.

Mecca brought in painter Gina Nagy Burns, who painted the white silk to mimic photos she and Sperling selected from photos of the pack ice in the Chukchi Sea taken the previous year. Burns painted lines of varying width in shades of dark gray accented with pops of bright turquoise, mimicking those that formed the cracks of water visible between the chunks of white ice. Sperling marveled at the precision of Burns' work. "There are no do-overs. It's a work of art, it's just incredible." Sperling practiced with the costume during New York City's winter, seeking out especially windy plazas that might mimic the conditions on her trip. Once she knew what the garment could do in blustery conditions, she created a solo in the studio called *Arctic Memory* to have a vocabulary of movement to draw from. The title is based on her idea of a "pre-memory." When she was actually on the sea ice, she used her solo as material but also improvised in the moment, depending on what the wind, the cold and her emotions at the time inspired her to do. To accommodate "the way that I dance, I had to move the way the wind blew me. I had to follow it, but it allowed me to be connected to the ice-scape."

Upon returning to New York, Sperling used the experience of dancing in the Arctic and her observations of the environment to inspire her next work, *Ice Cycle*. The footage of her dancing on the pack ice was made into a film called *Ice Floe*. "What the movement of the fabric does is show the movement of the ice over time. We didn't see the ice flowing. [Dancing] was like an echo of the landscape. It enabled me to have an identification with the ice."

Zepur Agopyan and Gundija Zandersona—*Contendō* (Premiere 2016)

An even more extreme example of the costume driving the dance is the experiment done by Zepur Agopyan, a young costume and set designer based in the United Kingdom. She set out to create a restrictive costume that would inspire choreography as the dancer fought against the costume. Beyond the desire to experiment with a costume-driven dance, her inspiration came from personal events in her own life that left her feeling restricted emotionally, physically and socially.

In addition to the psychological idea of restriction, she was also influenced by the work of Lisa Bufano. Bufano is a double amputee below the knee who creates performances using costume prosthetic pieces that give her a unique and different form, rather than mimicking a healthy body, and so making dance that no "able-bodied" performer would be able to do. Agopyan wanted to create a costume whose limitations would inspire unique choreography. She thought about how usually for dance costumes fabric must flow or stretch, decoration is placed where it is not uncomfortable, and freedom of movement is the ultimate goal. Instead, she sought to make something the opposite of this.

While the functionality of the costume was one of her goals, developing an interesting and aesthetically pleasing finished look was also a major component. "I wanted to create a costume that was free in design but not in performance." She sought to find a look for the costume that went along with the emotional and intellectual content of her idea, rather than just looking cool.

The costume she created, which won a costume design award in 2017 at World Stage Design in Taipei, was inspired by protective armor, medical corsetry and straitjackets. The deep red leather and quilted natural linen gave the garment a vintage look with a flavor of early sports equipment, or perhaps a superhero. Leather straps and buckles attached the leg and arm sections to the torso. The stitching in the quilted sections formed evenly spaced chevrons that followed the directionality of the body's musculature. Ratchets with metal cable attached shoulder to wrist and hip to ankle. They tightened gradually as the dancer moved. To make sure the choreography did not become undynamic, she left the midriff bare, so the torso could bend at will. The sleek helmet, molded in the red leather with linen accents, covered the top half of the face like an eyeless mask. While the performer did have some limited vision through the linen, the mask "cuts you off from the outside world and you are in a costume which is pulling you in, so it makes it an internal experience. Part of the performance . . . is [the dancer's] experience, even though we don't get to see it."

While it was not a term with which she was previously familiar, Agopyan learned that her experiment was part of a practice called *somatics*, being tuned to the body and its own sensory experiences. Somatics originates in traditional practices like yoga, and is used in dance and other physical performance, as well as in bodywork and therapy. Laban movement analysis and Alexander technique are examples of this field. Somatic costume is typically concerned with the physical and psychological experience for the practitioner more than with aesthetics. Costume may be used as part of an exercise for its physical properties, such as exploring what it is like to move wearing a tall headpiece or with padding around the body, training the wearer in awareness of certain movements or alignment.

As Agopyan pointed out "a costume cannot dance" and so she sought a choreographic collaborator. Gundija Zandersona's résumé seemed perfect, because in addition to her skills in contemporary dance, she had a background in gymnastics, and so the designer had less worry that the costume "might break her." Zandersona was intrigued by the idea of working from a costume as the source of her inspiration, something she had not tried before. She choreographed a dance that was a structured improvisation, based on the costume itself and some hints Agopyan gave her about the emotional state that inspired the costume's creation. "It was different from how I usually choreograph, because along with the costume there already was a very specific desired outcome—restriction of movements. Dancing in the costume was not comfortable, but that helped me form some of my choreographic choices. The headpiece created a separation between me and the audience and allowed me to be in my own space and focus on what I wanted to say."

In practice, the costume wasn't quite as restrictive as Agopyan had intended. "We as dancers are trained to find ways around obstacles and difficulties, so when the ratchets on the costume had tightened up and had made it harder to extend the leg, there were still many other choices for me to make to be able to dance," the choreographer noted. "It made me focus on the new choices that opened up because of wearing the costume, rather than limiting the existing ones." Instead, Zandersona made her movements purposely trigger the ratchets and cause them to tighten. Over the course of the performance, she created the appearance that the costume had "taken over."

The original intent was for the costume to provide its own soundtrack: the creaking of the leather, the clicking metallic sound of the ratchets, and the performer's breathing getting gradually more labored as the physically taxing costume took its toll would all reinforce the dancer's movements. However, it wasn't quite enough, and so they added a soundscape which was based on "wobbly sounds" recorded from cables hitting and vibrating.

LONG-TERM COLLABORATIONS

Both costume designers and choreographers seek to develop long-term collaborative relationships. While all artists also seek innovation and new partnerships, having a shared history provides many benefits. Conversations become easier. Many long-term collaborators develop a shorthand for communication and are able to reference past experiences to move to the desired outcome more efficiently and smoothly. Trust is also a key benefit, and artists feel more comfortable taking risks or proposing unusual ideas.

Some pairings of designer and choreographer lead to the development of a unique fusion style where the two artists become interdependent. Other times, artists will vary their collaborators depending on whose style suits the project best. Choreographer Kyle Abraham prefers to work with designer Karen Young for historically inspired pieces such as *The Gettin'* set in 1960s South Africa, while he gravitates to Reid & Harriet Design for gender-neutral looks like *When the Wolves Came In*, with both men and women in wigs.

Costume designer Christine Darch's long-term partnership with choreographer Julia Adam began because they clicked as both people and artists. Darch noted that "we have really similar taste. I think she'd agree that I could probably describe something to her and not have to draw it, or I could even show up to dress rehearsal with costumes and she'd probably like it."

When artists work together over a span of time, being able to evolve and change in compatible directions becomes paramount. Costume designer Liz Vandal worked for 20 years with choreographer Marie Chouinard. At first, Vandal felt that she and Chouinard were completely in sync, and she was able to "ride the wave" artistically. After a while, however, Vandal found that she had Chouinard's style down. She could easily do the abstracted costumes Chouinard preferred, but she hungered to try something different. Vandal wanted to explore, and to see Chouinard's dancers "in clothing." She tried out this new direction but she knew her ideas might not be well-received, so for the meeting with Chouinard she prepared two options. She brought costumes based on 1940s undergarments to try. When the choreographer was not receptive, the designer said "If you don't like it, no problem, I can bring in another set of costumes tomorrow. . . . I showed her the second version and she loved it, but it was [similar] to what we usually did. I wanted to bring a new spirit into our collaboration, but it was not possible."

ESSENTIAL COLLABORATION SKILLS
Communication

Clarity and openness are vital for good collaboration. Often, especially in such an abstract field as dance, relying only on words without accompanying visuals, whether image or gesture, can be a recipe for confusion. With verbal communication, both designers and choreographers should make sure that terminology is used in an unambiguous way. They will be clearest when they use examples, ask for definitions or refer to a supplementary visual aid. Words like bold, repetitive or postmodern can mean very different things to different artists. Visual communication is not inherently unambiguous either and intent should always be explained. Will the color shown be used throughout or as accents? Will a given movement phrase be the beginning of the dance or towards the middle?

Communication is also the key to problem-solving during the process. An open milieu where ideas can flow freely helps every working relationship. Honest, safe communication is necessary to navigating roadblocks, whether they be fitting the idea to the budget, developing and implementing the work on schedule, or making sure the lighting and costume look good together in the space. As choreographer Kyle Abraham said "I don't want people to say yes to me, I want them to tell me that something sucks and doesn't make any sense. I want to be able to say the same thing, in a non-offensive way."

Flexibility

One of the things that takes years to learn about collaborating is when to adapt and when to stand your ground. Young artists need to find the balance between being confident in their own ideas and being open to input from collaborators. If a designer's sketch makes a choreographer think the costume would not show the body enough, the designer should draw some alternate versions, but they might also try a more accurate sketch or even a prototype to explain how the fabric would in fact cling to the body in the original idea. If a choreographer wants a style that will be too time-consuming to make for the eight dancers in the work, before saying no a designer should look for ways to purchase a garment the shop can adapt. Both designers and choreographers can benefit from learning to truly consider and explore each option before rejecting it. And, both may find that adaptations based on input from others makes for a stronger idea than what they originally conceived.

Teamwork

Teamwork is essential for collaboration. To work as a team, everyone must know who all of the members are, their role and when their involvement begins. Are all the designers working on the dance together? Or is the choreographer working first with a costume designer and then bringing in lights much later? Is there a visual artist who has already created a backdrop? Are the dancers involved in shaping the choreography? Is there a star dancer who gets input into their costume? Will the dance be performed by multiple companies?

The chain of command for a project is also a part of teamwork. Any team needs a leader or facilitator—working truly as a leaderless peer group is difficult. Most typically the choreographer is the team leader, but sometimes the artistic director of the dance company or a producer or even a star is really the one with final say. How does the team communicate? Is it a group where lots of back and forth is desired, is every element discussed with every collaborator, or does everyone just get the "need to know" parts? No matter the leadership style, team members need to find a way to be inspired by, rather than just directed by, that person. And, the leader must find a way to encourage those working with them, not just direct or instruct. They should bring out creativity and make everyone feel like their contribution is vital to the project.

Case Study #4

The Wizard of Oz

CHOREOGRAPHER—SEPTIME WEBRE

**COMPANY—KANSAS CITY BALLET,
CO-PRODUCTION WITH COLORADO BALLET
AND THE ROYAL WINNIPEG BALLET**

PREMIERE DATE—OCTOBER 2018

DATE PHOTOGRAPHED—OCTOBER 2018

**PERFORMANCE VENUE—KAUFFMAN CENTER
FOR THE PERFORMING ARTS IN
KANSAS CITY, MO**

MUSIC—MATTHEW PIERCE

COSTUME DESIGN—LIZ VANDAL

SCENIC DESIGN MICHAEL B. RAIFORD

LIGHTING DESIGN—TRAD A. BURNS

PROJECTION DESIGN—AARON RHYNE

PUPPETRY DESIGN—NICHOLAS MAHON

Dorothy (Amanda DeVenuta) and Toto swept away by the tornado. The tornado is created by
flags carried by dancers and also with projections

James Kirby Rogers, Liang Fu, and Lamin Pereira dos Santos portray the three farmhands and Danielle Bausinger as Miss Gulch

A group of athletic men clad in yellow bodysuits forms geometric shapes as they leap into bold postures on a ramp, some with arms folded, others with fingers pointed disco-like to the sky. The decorative flaps of foam that cover their bodies like square feathers flutter as they *jeté*. To choreographer Septime Webre, the story of *The Wizard of Oz* is about taking an adventurous journey. To anchor his production, he sought a metaphor that would "embody the spirit of adventure that one has when you go down an uncharted path" and decided that the road should not be merely a piece of scenery, but also a group of men known as the Yellow Brick Roadies. Together with longtime collaborator, costume designer Liz Vandal, Webre transformed a tale best known on the page and the screen into his own classic yet updated story ballet. Webre had wanted for years to do an adaptation of the L. Frank Baum story but waited until he felt that he had something new to add. When he figured out an approach to the visuals, both the staging and the look of the characters, he knew the time was right. "The aha moment was figuring out the physicality of the secondary characters. What they might look like, dance like, and maybe even what the music might sound like. One of the things that makes *The Wizard of Oz* special is the ensemble of characters that Dorothy encounters—their outlandishness, their humanity, and the sense of fantasy that is made available in the book."

Webre began as a dancer, mainly in ballet. As a choreographer he started "as an abstract artist, influenced by Balanchine and Merce Cunningham . . . Abstraction was what serious choreographers tackled, not narrative work." Despite this pressure, he felt himself drawn to narrative, and sought to create his own contemporary style of story ballets. Webre had felt a yen for storytelling from a young age. As a child he wrote plays that starred his sister and directed the school talent show. At the young age of 30, he found himself the artistic director of the American Repertory Ballet and he realized that the company needed large-scale works to attract an audience. He began with classics, first trying his hand at *Romeo and Juliet*. However, in Webre's estimation, when choreographing from an existing ballet score, a composer such as Prokofiev "has already done 75 percent of the work. He has structured the dance and the choreographer just needs to make up steps to that glorious music." After working through a number of classics, Webre decided to make a ballet completely from scratch.

He chose *Alice in Wonderland*, which he created at the Washington Ballet in collaboration with Liz Vandal and composer Matthew Pierce. This 2012 ballet laid the groundwork for *The Wizard of Oz*,

and he used the same approach for both. He created a libretto in collaboration with Vandal, who served not only as costume designer but also as a dramaturg, helping him to see deeper into the characters and their function in the story. He worked with Pierce to decide the shape and style of the music for each section of the story.

Before he proposed the idea for *The Wizard of Oz* to his creative team and then to producers, Webre figured out a few more staging challenges to be sure he was ready. In addition to the Yellow Brick Roadies, other key ideas included using puppets and projections for the winged monkeys and representing Munchkinland with an "outrageous" color palette. After five collaborations with Pierce and 20 years of work with Vandal, the choreographer knew these two artists were essential to realizing his vision, and he made sure they were onboard. He needed the right score and costumes to support his energetic style of contemporary ballet, and so Webre included Pierce's music and Vandal's whimsical fashions in the package he pitched to potential producers. Webre considers his genre to be "ballet technique but with a contemporary air." He uses a lot of partnering, and men lift men as well as women. He feels that seeing the dancers really working with each other on stage helps the piece to "break through the formality of classical ballet."

As the project progressed, the team expanded. Puppet designer Nicholas Mahon and projection designer Aaron Rhyne proved equally vital to making the magic happen. Mahon created Winged Monkey puppets in forced perspective, rows of gradually smaller versions behind the front row of masked humans in Vandal's stern leather biker looks. He also designed a stylized yet lifelike Toto who wriggled and leapt across the stage alongside a puppeteer dressed like a Kansas farmhand. Rhyne created the tornado, the Wizard's disguises and many other effects.

Webre and Vandal have a unique working relationship that began on their first meeting 20 years ago. Webre recalls that he saw Vandal as his "artistic soulmate. We just clicked right away." Her recollection is that when they met for a preliminary chat, to see if they would want to collaborate, during the time they took to walk down the hall to her studio they had already designed a ballet. Their process is to brainstorm very quickly, and Vandal enjoys the great trust Webre has in her to take his ideas and translate them into costumes. After years of working together, she shows him sketches and swatches almost as a formality, knowing that she can create costumes and characters he will connect with. Her style is to work very intuitively. "I connect myself to what is right for the group. I am a giver and receiver of information. We can't be neutral receivers, though,

the wildly colored Munchkins

The "three ruffians" played by Angelin Carrant, Joshua Bodden, and Cameron Thomas. These characters pay homage to the Lollypop Guild in the film.

Toto (Jeremy Hanson puppeteer) gets to know a member of Munchkinland, Joshua Bodden.

The Wicked Witch (Bausinger) reaches for the ruby slippers

Munchkins in front of a floral set piece

The Scarecrow (Cameron Thomas) held aloft by the Roadies

the Yellow Brick Roadies

because of our personalities. I try to be as receptive as I can without any judgment, but I feel as it passes through my body."

Vandal has a distinctive style, originating from her roots in fashion and honed during her work designing costumes in many styles for prominent companies like Grands Ballets Canadiens de Montréal, Marie Chouinard, Mannheim Theater and Cirque du Soleil. She has worked in film and theater as well, but Vandal prefers to design for dance. Instead of delving into psychology with actors, she prefers the body in motion. "Dancers are in their bodies—if you make them beautiful and honor their bodies, they glow. You make them happy."

Being Canadian, Vandal had less history with *The Wizard of Oz* than most Americans do, and she decided to use her outsider perspective to her advantage. Although she was familiar with images from the classic film, she chose not to re-watch the movie or read the book. "I wanted to be intuitive about the story itself, be the one on the production team who was . . . feeling it on an intuition level instead of the background and history," Vandal says. She based her ideas on Webre's descriptions of how he saw the characters and the story. For the Cowardly Lion, Webre remembers that "they wanted to avoid him looking like an escapee from a bus and truck tour of *Cats*." Instead, they thought of a flashy, macho look that he put on like a mask to hide his tender nature underneath. And so, Vandal developed a glam-rock influenced style for him, his fur-trimmed sleeveless vest bedecked with jewelry. Starting with Vandal's idea of the straw as a Mohawk hairstyle, they came up with a lithe, punk-influenced Scarecrow. Tufts of raffia sprout here and there, accenting the mélange of colorful patchwork and darker stripes, sprinkled with buttons. From the movie, they kept the classic green skin for the Wicked Witch, but the rest of her costume originated from Vandal's riff on a crow. Green and purple accents lend highlight to the classic black expected of a witch, like the bird's iridescent feathers. Vandal adapted the standard witch hat into a hooked cone inspired by the crow's beak. As the dancer juts her chin out, the curve of the hat gracefully extends the line of her forehead. As choreographer and designer talked about the witch holding prisoners, the idea led them to a sexy look for her with (family friendly) fetish overtones of straps and buckles. The Winkies, the witch's back-up dancers, follow suit in a "Russian military meets fetish" design: severe coats with trailing skirts. They brandish riding crops, extending the line of their arms as they dance. Neither artist remembers exactly who came up with which ideas as they populated their world.

Each character moves in a way that suits their costume and character. The Lion poses like a rock star, lunging and leaping, trailing his tail like a microphone cord. The Scarecrow wobbles and dips, but also launches gracefully into the air, as light as if he were just filled with hay. His warm-toned colorful costume echoes his friendly demeanor as he greets each new acquaintance along the journey. The Wicked Witch and the Winkies perform choreography that takes full advantage of the long strips of fabric that radiate out when they spin. Both costumes and limbs form strong diagonals, giving the overall stage picture dynamic energy. Like the costumes, the choreography for the work mixes the classic with hints of pop culture and pure energy. Webre's modern ballet is punctuated by a wide variety of lifts and leaps, and the corps forms dynamic geometric shapes with their groupings. At times, the dance also picks up bits of swing dance, disco and even flossing, a current internet craze. And many cast members are literally airborne at times. The production makes generous use of flying harnesses—Dorothy flies into Oz, Glinda descends from above and the Scarecrow is tossed far into the air. And, of course the flying monkeys fly.

Vandal's designs do pick up on some of the classic images associated with the story, but she has also created her own unique worlds. For Kansas, she uses a palette of grays, both warm and cool, in shapes that evoke a deconstructed version of the early twentieth century. She cleverly brought in hints of the Oz characters to foreshadow the farm hands and crotchety neighbor becoming the Scarecrow, Tin Man, Lion and Witch. As she passes by on her bicycle, Miss Gulch wears a hat decorated with a crow and her tight bodice and full skirt echo the shape of the witch's dress. "I decided for some reason that [the ballet] would be all asymmetrical and I've never done that," the designer explained. "Normally I like symmetry." Dorothy is the only character in the ballet whose costume is symmetrical. Vandal sought to give each part of Oz its own unique look, contrasting angles and curves, juxtaposing matte against shiny. "I wanted people to travel as [Dorothy] is traveling, as if it's different planets." From Webre's request that Munchkinland be a garden of flowers, she created rounded costumes in a riot of color and graphic pattern. During design meetings, they talked about Emerald City being angular and faceted and glittery. The strong triangular shape of emerald facets reminded both of them of the broad shoulders and strong lines of the 1980s. However, Vandal made sure to translate the vibe without distorting the dancers' shoulder shape, to preserve the lines of the ballet. Vandal described the overall effect of Emerald City as "like a disco ball planet. The lighting [by designer Trad A. Burns] makes it all come alive." The music, which follows a more symphonic style for most of the ballet, veers to a jazzy tone to support the look and the disco dance moves. Vandal's goal with

The Wicked Witch (Elysa Hotchkiss) and Glinda (Taryn Mejia) face off in Munchkinland

Glinda descends, bringing snow to stifle the poppies

the corps dancers as poppies

Dancers in the faceted costumes of Emerald City

Dorothy and friends ham it up in Emerald City

all her designs is to give each dancer a "sexiness," which for her means a sense of power and beauty, and the feeling of honoring and being "in the body."

Vandal drew on her years of experience to choose the right fabrics and create silhouettes that not only show character and scene, but also work with partnering and lifts. She created garments that moved well with the body, such as the streamer-like skirt on the Wicked Witch and the poppies' buoyant circle-skirts. She used techniques that she learned at Cirque du Soleil designing the insect-inspired circus *OVO* to create unusual body shapes, support headpieces and handle athletic movement in harnesses. She also made sure that the dancers had ample rehearsal time in the specialized shapes so the witch could get used to spinning in her asymmetrical hat and the munchkins could work in donuts of padding around the waist and spirals of foam over the shoulder.

The influence of the costume design on the production was magnified by the fact that Webre had to change set designers mid-stream. Set designer Michael B. Raiford joined the team after the costume sketches were finished, and he took his cues from the colors and shapes Vandal developed. He echoed the graphic colors and patterns of her costumes in the giant geometric flowers that fly in for Munchkinland, and the dynamic, angular sunbursts in the Witch's castle complement the swirling strips of the Winkies' Cossack-like coats.

Webre explains how "the DNA of the costumes worked themselves into not just the set design but also the steps." As an example, the "Yellow Brick Roadies make a lot of graphic shapes in the air that mirror the costumes themselves." He began choreographing the ballet after the costumes were completely designed. He prefers to work in this way, because knowing the costume illuminates the character and helps him develop the way that they move. As his career has progressed, he has been using more "virtuosic technique . . . not to impress audiences, but to live life where it's risky and bold. If those are used properly, they are metaphors for the strength of the characters." A good example of this is the three "ruffians," Webre's homage to the Lollipop Guild in the movie. They are three athletic men in fluorescent colors with flanges protruding from hip and shoulder. Their David Bowie-influenced shape helped him develop "cocky and preening" choreography for them. In most cases, he was able to create moves that worked with the costume. After they got to dress rehearsal, if something needed adjustment, sometimes he tweaked the choreography, other times the costume was adapted.

No matter how many years of experience a designer or choreographer has, no one can foresee all of the technical demands, and sometimes adjustments do have to be made. However, veterans know what is worth changing, and what can be easily fixed or adapted. Vandal's original inspiration for Glinda was a soap bubble. For her first entrance, she wanted the dancer to hold an umbrella that would support a full bubble of iridescent costume over her head with only the legs visible. However, the aerial wires that flew her in did not work with the costume—getting the bubble off gracefully when the good witch landed was too difficult. And so, Vandal changed her design to an umbrella-shaped tutu made of petals of fabric, adorned with shiny bubble-like discs appliqued to the surface. The ensemble women in the Emerald City number wear stiff crinolines that give their outfits the geometry and sharpness of the faceted aesthetic the designers developed. One of Webre's partnering moves caused the male dancers to be uncomfortably scratched by the netting. However, that moment wasn't essential to the dance, and so he chose to just adjust the choreography. While Vandal's original design for Dorothy was for both a gray costume and a colored one, there was not time for her to change before she landed in Oz, and so they chose to have her start in the colored outfit, rather than adding to the dance to fill time while she changed. The soft purple and blue of her dress are harmonious with the grays of Kansas, and the audience does not sense anything missing.

Webre credits Vandal with teaching him to go deeper into the field of design, how "to mine the ideas with dramaturgy." He had not been exposed to dance that does this kind of dramaturgical work. For him, "dance is more kinetic, [and design conversations tend to focus on] technique and general atmosphere, it doesn't dig as deep as in visual art or theater." While at the beginning of his career, his primary goal was for "things to look cool," he now finds a detailed design process an indispensable part of his choreography. A successful design "makes the dance better and contributes to the ideas coming across . . . it elevates the dance, [rather than] just complementing it."

The Tin Man (Dillon Malinski) dancing in front of a projection representing the Great and Terrible Oz

The Wicked Witch of the West (Bausinger) intimidates Dorothy (DeVenuta) as the Winkies look on

The Wicked Witch of the West (Elysa Hotchkiss)and members of the corps portraying Winkies

Dorothy and friends in front of a projection of the moon

Dorothy with the Witch's broom

The Tin Man (Malinski) waits to be rescued in front of corps dancers portraying trees

The Flying Monkeys. The front row are dancers and the back rows are puppets in forced perspective held aloft on poles by dancers.

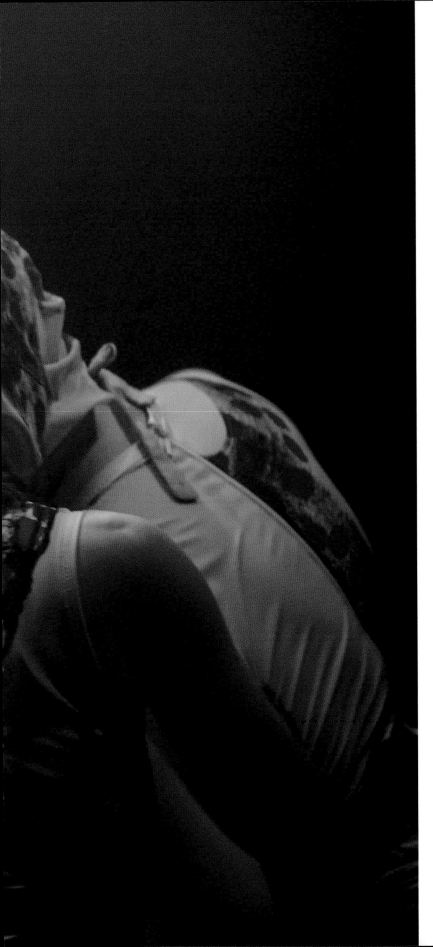

4

The Process—
Foundations:
Developing Initial
Concepts

Starting a project can be the most challenging part, but also the most exciting. This chapter explores ways that both choreographers and designers spark their own creation processes, and the initial stages of their collaborative dialog that will continue through the completion of the work. Different styles and methods are delineated here, but most artists use more than one of these, and often overlap several at any given moment. The systems that artists use to develop a project are as varied as the artists themselves.

FINDING THE CHOREOGRAPHIC IDEA

Choreographer Nicole Haskins pointed out that, just like in a scientific investigation, artists should begin a collaboration without a set outcome in mind. Scientists follow the data and don't try to predict the conclusion. Artists should also follow where the exploration takes them, both when making choreography and when collaborating with designers. This leads to a "wonderful back and forth where . . . [the outcome is] exactly what I wanted but not at all what I thought I wanted initially."

Clearly there is no right way to come up with an idea. Choreographers draw from all kinds of experiences in their lives: books they read, photos they see in a magazine or emotions circling in their heads. Typically, pieces are based on a combination of influences.

dancers perform Ingri Fiksdal's *STATE* (for more information, see Case Study #3)

And of course, music inspires dances, whether it triggers a complex narrative, a political statement, or pure movement. When choreographer Amy Seiwert starts a piece, music is her jumping off point, but pinpointing the true basis for her ideas is difficult. "I like to fall in love with a piece of music first, and that will give me images, and then I go from there. [My creative process is] so abstract. I am pulling in inspiration from so many sources: visual art, poems, etc. It all comes together in this crazy soup. It's rarely a straight line."

While most typically a choreographer initiates a work, many dances do start from commissions. This can simply mean that a choreographer is hired to create a new piece for a dance company or festival, with no set content, music or theme, but a commission can also be more specific. A ballet company might hire someone to do a new version of *The Nutcracker* or a contemporary company might commission a work as part of a thematic concert on the anniversary of women's suffrage.

Dance Inspired by Music

While plenty of choreographers choose or commission music after starting the creation of a piece, or even after finishing it, music is a very common beginning point for creating dance. Choreographers relate to so many aspects of the music—rhythm and phrasing, tempo, mood, genre and sometimes narrative content if there are lyrics.

Nicole Haskins—*The Poetry of Being* for Smuin Ballet (Premiere 2017)

The work of choreographer Nicole Haskins is grounded in traditional ballet, with the women in pointe shoes. She aims to make ballets with a "human feel," rather than give them an explicit contemporary twist. The beauty and expressive quality of the music in the first two movements of Tchaikovsky's *Souvenir de Florence* spoke to her, and she wanted to use them in a work. But figuring out how to make a cohesive structure from just the first half of the sextet for strings proved to be a challenge. "The first movement is very intense at times, layered and aggressive, bombastic and full of energy. The second movement is very serene, very calm, with gloriously beautiful strings. But the two on their own, you might not know they were from the same score." Without all four movements of the composition, which would make the varying styles between movements feel more coherent, she had to find her own way to unify her dance. She felt the two movements were too linked to

simply make a standalone piece to each movement. Instead, she decided that "I really had to over-exaggerate that there is this shift."

As she spent more time with the music, she realized that the divergence in style of the two sections *was* her theme. "The music was touching on the theme of this duality . . . two sides to everything . . . I had this idea of the two sides of the dancer." And she realized that the design elements—costume and lighting—would be an important way to connect the movements. She envisioned a specific shade of cobalt blue for the piece. "It's a striking color. [Blue is] one of the few colors that doesn't evoke too much—red is so intense. It's the only color that created an intensity but still a softness." In the first section, she had costume designer Susan Roemer put all the dancers in blue except one couple in nude. The idea of the nude was "not trying to be naked but exposed, vulnerable." Then to transition to the second section, the couple in nude performed a duet, and the blue color became light bathing the floor, "ethereal like they are floating on the blue." Next, all the dancers switched to nude costumes and "everything connected like they are different sides of the dancers that we are seeing." To conclude the piece, the couple from the duet returned in blue costumes, which she thought would "feel like they were really the only ones there all along, even though the other dancers are other [emotions] that were still attached to them."

Dance Evolved from Text or Narrative

A common starting point for dance is a text or narrative idea. This can be a dance that portrays a storyline overtly, where dancers play specific characters and the audience follows a plot from beginning to end. Or a choreographer may use a text, whether poem, novel or film, to inspire a partially or completely abstracted work. The audience may pick up themes or references from the source material, or they might simply experience the mood, dynamics or movement patterns the text inspired in the choreographer while remaining unaware of the source.

The story *The Yellow Wallpaper* by Charlotte Perkins Gilman, for instance, which is about a depressed Victorian woman confined to her room who imagines the pattern in the wallpaper is a person trying to get out, might inspire a choreographer to do a piece about insanity and gender roles. Or it could lead to a piece where the dancers actually seem to be inhabiting the walls. There could be characters representing the woman and her husband, or a group of dancers could be doing choreography that embodies the feeling of being trapped. The piece could reference the nineteenth century through music and costume, or not at all.

Jack Ferver—*Chambre* at The Fisher Center at Bard College (Premiere 2014)

Jack Ferver is a choreographer who works in a theatrical style, but does not like to be defined by the term *dance theater*, nor *performance art*. "I am making pieces. I am an emotional formalist and my medium is live art." He explained that "I make these performance works that utilize various forms—dance and theater, also humor, horror, political structures, the things we do to each other. I look at all of those things as forms." Ferver created a piece based on the 1947 play *The Maids* by Jean Genet, and also on the historical event that provided Genet's original source material—two sisters who were maids and killed their employer in the 1930s. His piece, *Chambre*, was set in contemporary New York but also made references to the socialist France of the original. To explore the role of Madame, he connected her character to "the narcissism of a millennial like Lady Gaga. As well as my own narcissism. I wasn't setting out to indict anyone without indicting myself." As in Genet's original, he cast men as the maids. "The most simplistic way of reading my work is it plays with gender, sexual orientations and class disparity."

In collaboration with visual artist Marc Swanson, Ferver created a work staged in an art gallery, its set more like an installation than typical scenery. Doorways and windows that do not actually form walls framed the space, festooned with swags of drapery and delicate glittering chains. The space was fancy, artificial and somewhat empty. As he brought costume into the mix, he gave the following directive to frequent collaborator Reid Bartelme: "I said I picture them in a skin they are really uncomfortable in. I want maid costumes made out of skin. [Costumes] that *are* their skin but it's weak—they are not safe under it." Bartelme developed translucent flesh-toned maid dresses, traditional in shape but fragile in appearance, that showed the male bodies underneath.

Dance Evolved from an Emotional State or Exploring a Theme

Many choreographers make pieces that explore their own current state of mind, whether primarily focusing on an emotion or exploring a motif that has been peeking into the edges of their consciousness. Sometimes it is a theme they plan to investigate at the outset, other times the piece is in development before they figure out what its through-line is.

Amy Seiwert and Sandra Woodall—*Broken Open* for Smuin Ballet (Premiere 2016)

Amy Seiwert created a contemporary ballet work called *Broken Open*, which explored "the idea that you can take something ugly—emotionally, physically—and turn it into your own definition of beauty." She read about a woman who had a mastectomy and then had the scars made into decorative tattoos on her chest, which resonated with her personally as she has a family history of breast cancer. It also reminded her of visiting Berlin not long after the Berlin Wall was torn down. "I love it when you see a building from the nineteenth century next to one built in 1972 and they share a window because half that other building was bombed. Instead of tearing it all down, one leads to another." A lot of the buildings were decorated with graffiti "and it was amazing. Some of it looked like graffiti and some was this incredible art. And on these buildings that might have been torn down." She saw a parallel between these, and to the creation of art generally, in taking pain and suffering and using it to create something beautiful.

While the final dance is abstracted, and the audience does not think about walls or surgery, the costumes, by Sandra Woodall, retain some overt elements of the thematic exploration. Woodall took the graffiti idea further by looking at how the designs on walls build up layer on top of layer over time. The final product is the boldly adorned dancers in a stark 'white box'—neutral colored lighting in a white space, letting the transformed bodies take central stage. The dancers wear costumes printed with unique layered graffiti designs separated by solid black portions. "Every garment is different in terms of the design and how it's placed, but together it created a whole wall," Woodall said. "In the case of [Seiwert's] piece it should be very clean and clear what the body is doing. [We are] not creating different characters, it's a piece that is abstract. So, in that case it's a minimal costume but it's . . . well graffiti-ed."

Dance Based on Pure Movement

For some choreographers, the choreographic movement in a dance is not only the end product, but the process as well. Many works explore the gestures, groupings or rhythms formed by the dancers' bodies. These dances are a more abstract art form, which do not link to narrative, emotion or theme, other than potentially in the mind of the viewer.

dancers from Bruce Wood Dance perform *Follow Me* by Bruce Wood, costume design by John Ahrens, lighting design by Tony Tucci.

Liz Gerring—*Horizon* for Liz Gerring Dance Company (Premiere 2015)

Choreographer Liz Gerring starts thinking of her dances visually. A self-described "postmodern formalist with a contemporary athletic vocabulary," she imagines bodies moving in space, executing steps or forming shapes in her signature physical style. Sometimes she starts a new piece with dancers and numbers—for instance choosing to do a quartet of men. Her first ideas come from "the ingredients: how many dancers, where they are in space, how they are moving, what different groupings. Rather than a narrative idea I might be trying to express. The form [of the dance] has meaning to it but that meaning may be different for each person." She evolves her work through improvisation in the studio and is influenced by the dancers in the cast. "Every piece is made of specific bodies and specific personalities and that will often influence ideas that I have."

She does use music as she works on the dance, but just as a placeholder. Once the work is choreographed, she has composer Michael J. Schumacher come in and "score the dance" afterwards. "We may talk about ideas beforehand, but I make the dance and then he writes the music for the dance." In parallel with her process of creating an abstract dance, about movement rather than narration or emotion, she keeps her visuals in an aesthetic that is more art gallery than typical stage performance. "Lighting is more about lighting the space than lighting the piece. The sound and the music work together to create an environment in which the dance takes place, almost like an installation, like you are installing this atmosphere and people are moving in that." She feels that the costumes should also be a part of this environment, rather than separating the dancers out of the surround.

"I envisioned a piece with a lot of activity, lots of layers of movement phrases, in contrast to [her previous work] *Glacier*, that was more austere. Robert [Wierzel] envisioned light with a lot of color and movement." Gerring credits production designer Wierzel with the idea to bring in bold color for *Horizon*, which is not typical in her work. Costume designer Liz Prince followed Wierzel's lead and tested different color combinations on the dancers. Gerring appreciated the way that Prince experimented in order to come up with a combination that looked best on each dancer. During the residency they tried the whole cast in yellow, but the final look she created was a variety of solid-colored pieces: yellow, red, blue and gray, punctuated by one dancer in a boldly color-splashed printed top that brought all the tones together. While the dance itself remained very abstract, Gerring appreciated the touch that Prince brought to the work. "It's nice to sometimes see dancers as people and not just dancers."

Dance Created from a Commission

Many dances are created for commissions—these can be to join a thematic series like a concert about global warming, to commemorate an event like the fiftieth anniversary of the Summer of Love, or to choreograph *The Carnival of the Animals* for a symphony as part of a concert aimed at a family audience. Frequently, a commission can be inspiring to an artist, nudging them to create work on themes or in styles that they would not ordinarily pursue.

Joy Bollinger and John Ahrens—Bruce Wood's *Follow Me* for Bruce Wood Dance (Premiere 2004)

Bruce Wood received a phone call from his agent out of the blue. When he heard the proposal, he thought it was a joke. The United States Army wanted to commission him to create a dance. The company recently revived their late founder's work as part of a Veteran's Day timed concert. As Wood recounted in a film shown before the dance, he wondered if the army knew he was a "liberal, democrat, artistic guy?" But in fact, the US Army Brigade from Fort Benning wanted a dance for the opening of the RiverCenter in Columbus, Georgia. In the video, he described himself as a "child of the 1960s and 70s" and noted that he had preconceived notions about the army. Although the idea unsettled him, he gamely went to the base to do research and learn more. As the company's long-time costume designer John Ahrens recalled, "Bruce was very apprehensive—he didn't know what was going to happen when they [the dance company] got there." Wood participated in Ranger training and he even jumped out of a helicopter. After spending time with the soldiers, he realized that they had a lot of common ground. The piece he created sought neither to glorify nor protest war, but instead centered on the experiences of soldiers and their families at home.

Joy Bollinger, current artistic director of the company, who danced in the original version of the work, recalled that "what stood out to [Wood] was the brotherhood. Their protection for each other was life-changing for them. Their bravery and pain and grief led to the brotherhood they developed . . . Bruce said, 'I don't know what it's like to go to war, but I do know what it's like to lose someone. And to feel that need to hold onto other people and protect other people,' so that's what he made it about."

The work is done in a ballet-influenced modern style. The piece has sections with just the four male dancers as soldiers that use drill-like gestures to portray training and then a harrowing although abstracted experience in battle. Three men also perform duets with three women, a lyrical tribute to the bonds they have and the bonds they leave. Bollinger described the ending of the piece, where the four men partner and lift each other, their arms intertwining, bodies supporting each other's weight. "The final section is the four men together. Not just to fight—their job is to take care of each other. You draw your strength from those other people you are with." A square of light on the floor defines the performance space for the piece. Even when the company is touring, they recruit actual veterans to stand in uniform onstage but just outside of the square. "At the end they come into the light and salute. It gives me goosebumps every time," Bollinger said. Wood's own words about the dance were "I'm successful when the dance makes [the veterans] remember how they felt."

Creating a Dance for Specific Dancers

Often the dancers who will perform a piece significantly influence the work. The type of influence ranges from how individuals interpret the steps or movements to being part of the actual inspiration for the work. A work can be created to showcase a certain dancer's (or group of dancers') personality, movement style, physical ability or appearance. Dancers may be cast for what they bring to an intended piece, or the dancers may exert influence more subtly in terms of how they shape the movement during the development process.

Bryan Arias—*Live, Love, Laugh* for Bruce Wood Dance (Premiere 2019)

Bryan Arias creates his contemporary choreography in the studio while he works with the dancers. Most of his work is created as commissions for specific dance companies that bring him in as a guest artist. When he starts work with a new set of dancers, he spends the first two days giving them structured improvisations.

"I don't come in with movement prepared at all. I like to tap into a sense of flow, I work a lot quicker that way." As he watches the dancers work, he begins to get choreographic ideas based on the individual dancers. "It's like people-watching—you start to imagine things as you watch them move." If he sees a pair or group of dancers that have chemistry, he may start to develop sections of the piece that "test that chemistry." He creates what he terms "points of connection" or "landmarks" as he works. He also creates a playlist of music and puts it on in the background during the improvisation. This way he can quickly realize whether or not the music selections will work for the given situation. He also uses the music as a guide to demonstrate to the dancers the ambiance he imagines for the work. He "chooses minimalistic music so we can fill in, color it, shape it." As they work together in the studio, he gradually shapes the piece into sections that complement each other and revolve around a thematic whole.

He begins each work with a variation on the same question: "What does it mean to be human?" He created a piece for Bruce Wood Dance entitled *Live, Love, Laugh.* He explained the title as "live like this is your one shot, love like you mean it . . . and laugh—don't take it all too seriously." While he did not want to be too literal in interpreting themes, he looked for ways the ideas could translate into movement. "What does this idea mean physically? Laughter makes you soft, makes you relax, be receptive to others. Take into consideration who the other person is." He always wants the dancers' humanity to be what is seen on stage. "When I work with dancers, we talk about intentions . . . It is abstract but we emphasize authenticity and honesty. When you allow the dancers to be that way it becomes completely human."

FINDING THE COSTUME DESIGN IDEA

The designer's work follows a path that gradually reveals itself, based on the choreographer's ideas and movements and on input from other designers and collaborators. Each designer travels this path differently, although they usually pass through many of the same steps: research, fabrics, sketching and fittings. In order to travel, something has to spark the journey and start the designer on their exploration.

Responding to the Choreographer's Concept

Many designers respond best to initial verbal ideas or conversations. Their job is to translate emotions or concepts into shape, line and color. Karen Young likes to take time to digest ideas. Even if choreography is not at all set yet, she prefers to come into the process very early. "Then I can bring ideas in . . . It's nice to have some time to bounce ideas off each other, then sit with it for a while and let it dwell. How you are going to bring in all the layers and the languages of what you are talking about. How exactly you are going to bring all the elements together."

Mary Jo Mecca—*Escher/Bacon/Rothko* by Zvi Gotheiner for Zvi Dance (Premiere 2015)

Choreographer Zvi Gotheiner developed a piece about three twentieth-century artists. He sought to explore the themes in the artists' works, rather than visually translating the images in the paintings. For the section on Francis Bacon, he began with the artist's images of wrestlers, in order to deconstruct what it is to be a man in society, living a life that appears "normal" on the outside. Gotheiner talked with costume designer Mary Jo Mecca about the competing pulls to be a "gentleman" and then the "savage behavior" that lies below. Mecca knew the choreographer intended for the men to end the section by wrestling, so she had a clear basis for what the second look needed to be. But to figure out the first look, she ruminated on the "proper English gentleman." She tried to create a generalization of the look of the average working man. "I knew how I wanted them to end and worked backwards. I thought it would be interesting to have them pulled together in a shirt and tie and then have them bust out of it." She worked with the choreographer to integrate the costume change into the work. Neither of them wanted it to be a conventional change, or to feel like a striptease. "It was like the unraveling of respectability . . . you didn't even know it was happening—like it was falling off of them." Mecca really likes to find inspiration in this way—to riff on the choreographer's initial conceptual ideas. "He gives me those images and I can fly with that. It sends me into designer heaven. He speaks in emotions. I get that into a form."

Responding to the Movement and Music

Many designers start with the music. As they listen, they gauge their emotional response and use it to see colors or feel shapes. The abstraction of music can help many designers to take an artistic leap and to find something that connects with the piece without being too literal. Other designers use a similar process but respond to the dancers' movements in rehearsal. Rather than thinking primarily about the thematic content of the piece, they react to the flow and gesture of the bodies as they watch.

dancers from Bruce Wood Dance perform *Follow Me* by Bruce Wood.

Costume designer Emily Morgan spends a lot of time looking at visual art. When she visits galleries and museums, she compiles a library of images in her mind. Then, as she watches dancers in rehearsal, "I tend to think of color and movement simultaneously . . . When I am watching a piece, my brain will do a little hyperlink to something that I have seen . . . It will start to feel like I'm seeing color and shape simultaneously—as if I'm looking at a painting but I'm actually watching a dance piece."

Sandra Woodall likes to attend rehearsals and sketch the dancers as she watches. While she also has extended conversations with the choreographer about ideas, and trades image research back and forth, her experience has taught her that "when a choreographer really begins to say what he means is when he gets into the studio." And so, she attends rehearsals with a sketchbook and a camera. "The way that I get into it is to begin to draw the figure. Then that way I see the shapes [the choreographer] is creating, and flow and movement." She first concentrates on drawing the bodies of the dancers. "Then after that, I begin to develop the clothing. It really comes from the form." She also takes photos of the dancers and uses those to lead her to costume ideas.

Holly Hynes—*Liturgy* by Christopher Wheeldon for New York City Ballet (Premiere 2003)

Costume designer Holly Hynes is "inspired in the beginning by the music and what is says to the choreographer, but also by what it says to me. Shutting your eyes and imagining as you listen—maybe that morphs or changes or gives you some other new direction." She designed a *pas de deux* for choreographer Christopher Wheeldon. "I remember Chris saying, 'I don't really have an idea yet, but when I listen to the music it has a war reference.'" And so, Hynes spent time with a recording of the music, *Fratres* by Arvo Pärt, letting her mind's eye lead her. As she listened, Hynes envisioned the male dancer as war and the female dancer as peace. To find an abstract translation of this metaphor for modern ballet costumes, she decided to first focus on very specific color choices. She decided to juxtapose a "dark, blood-saturated color" for the man and a dove gray for the woman. Wheeldon liked this direction, and Hynes developed shapes for each dancer, continuing the war and peace idea. For the woman, dancer Wendy Whelan, Wheeldon told Hynes that "he thought the more skin showing, the more vulnerability she would have." And so, Hynes developed a leotard that gave a lot of bareness, using cutouts with a "sculptural, almost

wing shape to it." In the finished design, the bottom half of the leotard is a solid brief but then the gray fabric, supported by nude mesh, arcs up from the waist, curves across the breast and then tapers out across the shoulder blade. The man's costume, a tank unitard, is all in dark red but has cutouts of opaque fabric curving across the torso, also supported by transparent mesh. Hynes was pleased and surprised when she noticed that in the finished ballet there were times that Whelan's arms echoed the wing-like shapes of the costume.

Finding Inspiration When the Choreography is Not Yet Started

While most designers prefer to develop their designs knowing as many of the variables as possible, some venues require designs well before the choreography has been significantly developed, often due to build schedules in the costume shop. If the designers can't know the full picture—how the dancers will move, what the overall structure of the choreography will be, what the lighting and scenery will be—they have to find a way to work just from detailed conversations with choreographers.

Reid & Harriet Design—*Une Autre Passion* by Pontus Lidberg for Les Ballets du Grand Théâtre de Genève (Premiere 2017)

Design team Reid Bartelme and Harriet Jung were hired to design a new ballet with choreographer Pontus Lidberg. Six months ahead, well before Lidberg was to begin rehearsals, they had to do a design presentation for the producers. They learned from the choreographer that he was using Bach's *Saint Matthew Passion* as the music but was not planning to follow the narrative in its libretto, just use it for a broader view. The dancers would not portray specific characters. And so, to figure out a basis for their design, they reached back to their training at the Fashion Institute of Technology. Bartelme explained that "we approached it like a piece from school. We did a mood board and put together fabrics—like a 22-person fashion collection to present to this opera house." Jung added that "what actually helped was we had worked with the choreographer before and we knew his aesthetic, what he likes, what his work is usually like. So that also informed us." To supplement that, they asked him general questions to gauge his overall vision for the piece. Whether or not he imagined certain colors? Did he envision a uniform, or each dancer as unique?

EXPANDING THE IDEA: CONCRETE CHOREOGRAPHY IDEAS

Choreographers evolve their initial concepts into movement phrases, and gradually put together the overall structure of their dance. As they do this, designers follow along, developing their own ideas as the dance itself takes shape. Gradually, the movement and costumes, as well as other aspects like music, lighting, scenery or projections, go from impulses to fully fleshed ideas.

How do Choreographers Evolve their Dance?

Choreographers expand their ideas using a variety of approaches. Most choreographers have preferred methods, but those may vary over their body of work. Liz Gerring does not like to work alone—she creates her ideas on her dancers in rehearsal. At the outset, she generates the ideas, and "they are like note-takers as I am improvising or moving." She does not have them create any of the movement. "I am sketching it, and they are turning it into a live painting." However, as the dance progresses, she does get ideas from watching the bodies of the dancers as they move. After Paul Vasterling has his initial idea for a piece, he then works in the studio with just one dancer for a while before working with the entire cast.

Dwight Rhoden sees the dancers as more of a direct influence. "I am one of those choreographers that is really affected by the dancer that is in front of me. I walk into the room with a set of ideas and directions and things I want to talk about, but I don't walk in with everything completely worked out. I am very influenced by the dancers in rehearsal. They are the link to finding [things] out. As I'm digging deeper into a concept, they are the instrument that really helps me mine whatever it is that I am looking to explore." Rhoden lets the movement be the main driver of his ideas. In fact, he often chooses music at the outset but doesn't play it in rehearsal for quite a while. "I also feel that the movement itself has to speak in the way that I want to before I actually put it to music."

Not surprisingly for a choreographer who is also a visual artist (a photographer), Trey McIntyre begins his dances by envisioning the big picture. "What does the environment on the stage look like?" Prior to working with dancers on choreography in the studio, "I want to know the bones, the architecture and ribcage of the work. What is the emotional and dynamic journey of the piece?" He has his own particular methods to pull together visual stimuli into an idea for a dance. "I like doing that in kind of random ways. Looking at animals and how they move, thinking about Amy Winehouse another day, so that there is this treasure chest of things to draw from when I'm in the studio, and costume is a very big part of that."

Bryan Arias evolves his work by presenting a series of challenges to the dancers and to himself in rehearsal. "When we start getting comfortable, I present a new [one]," he explained. These challenges may be physical or intellectual explorations. In an upcoming piece he is developing for Ballett Basel, he plans to explore some costume-based challenges. The dancers will be dressed in jackets, and he wants to try "taking the biggest jacket from the tallest guy and putting it on the smallest girl in the cast. Or all the guys in the group take off their jackets and put all of them onto the smallest girl—can she put them all on? How would she take them off? Would she collapse under them?" He uses this strategy based on how he functioned best as a dancer, prior to becoming a choreographer. He doesn't share all the ideas for a piece with the dancers at the outset. "I felt waiting to know certain things worked well for me as a dancer, it kept a wheel or an engine running."

EXPANDING THE IDEA: CONCRETE COSTUME IDEAS

Once the designer has the initial inspiration, what comes next? How can they start to transform a concept, an emotion or the movement of bodies in space into clothing? Designers have many ways to expand and develop ideas, to spark an internal conversation or one with collaborators. Research, drawing, looking at materials—many methods can help to translate concepts into something wearable.

Research: Verbal and Visual Ideas

Research is a crucial component for many designers, and for many choreographers as well. This might be conceptual research, exploring texts that relate to themes in the piece. They may study psychology, history or politics that relates to the material being developed. Certainly, if a choreographer is working from material like this, most designers will want to read or explore the same source material. Research may also be visual: browsing paintings, photographs or sculptures. This exploration may be done to spark or expand ideas, or to find a more concrete way to communicate ideas they already have, to serve as metaphor for their initial impulses.

While most types of research are relatively straightforward, sometimes research can take unusual forms. Designer Mary Jo Mecca worked on a piece that planned to use projections. The production team learned that the Museum of Modern Art had a visiting exhibit using 360-degree projections, and she, the lighting designer and the choreographer took a field trip. "We laid on the pillows watching this projection. I watched how the video was laying on people's clothing while they were walking around. I got the idea from that how it would look, what would work."

Sandra Woodall—*Ask Me* by Adam Houghland for Smuin Ballet (Premiere 2015)

In Sandra Woodall's initial conversations with choreographer Adam Houghland for the piece *Ask Me*, he mentioned that he was drawn to exploring the dancers themselves, as people. "He told me he was really interested in the way dancers . . . change when they leave rehearsal. They have practice clothes on, and then they change a little to go home and finish their day, and then you see them at a gallery or party afterwards." Woodall decided to use this as inspiration, but not too directly. Instead she decided, with the choreographer's permission, to talk to the dancers and use that as research. "I was interested in interviewing dancers not about clothes but about themselves. I would design something based on my impressions and thoughts." She asked them about their past and future, their likes and dislikes, but nothing about their taste in clothing. "From that I designed a garment for each person that tried to capture their essence." This echoed the choreography, which was also to be based on the individuals. Each night the set of garments on stage was different because casting shifted as the company performed different days.

Melanie Watnick—*Hey-Hay, Going to Kansas City* by Donald McKayle for Kansas City Ballet (Premiere 2008)

Costume designer Melanie Watnick designed a work for choreographer Donald McKayle called *Hey-Hay, Going to Kansas City*, about the jazz movement in the 1930s and 40s. McKayle, born in 1930, had memories of the era, and recalled his mother getting dressed up to go out on the town. Watnick recalled that McKayle "really understood clothing and textiles . . . and music. We started to develop that piece around fashion history and the silhouette of the time period." He was fluent in the language of clothing: "a two-tone wingtip, a peekaboo shoe." She used research into the time, photographs and vintage clothing, to get ideas for details, colors and patterns that would give the desired feeling for the work. Together, Watnick and McKayle mined the research for ways to give each dancer an individual personality, using details from the clothing of the time. The dance had sections set to different jazz compositions, "one having a drunken loungey feel, or a playful section. Or a duet with a man and woman going out on the town dressed to the nines." Watnick wanted to ensure that the ballet dancers "felt like real people rather than 'I have a 40s dress and a bun.'" She designed costumes that were "cut like clothes, in prints of the era." The dancers wore ballroom shoes rather than ballet slippers, and she got special permission from the company to use period hairstyles and hats. However, as she finalized the designs for the piece, she made sure that period realism was not the only focus. She had worked quite a bit with McKayle previously and she knew "he's always been about color and joy. I knew the colors would be elevated, and I also have known that in dance even if people say 'realism' the color and details are amplified, especially for a joyous piece . . . it's dialed up, like musical theater."

Trying Out and Refining Ideas with Drawings

Most designers use sketching or drawing as part of their process, whether on paper or digitally. Some do realistic detailed drawings, while others make rough squiggles, working out ideas for shapes. The sketches also become a basis for conversation with collaborators, and a blueprint to be handed off to the costume-makers, but the initial sketching time is often just for the designer. Picturing the costume in one's head is rarely enough even for experienced designers. Most need to see images on the page to be able to react to the idea and refine it. Others find the act of sketching to *be* the act of creation, and the details manifest themselves as the drawing takes shape.

Some designers draw while listening to music, others while watching dancers in rehearsal. Some go to sketching sooner in the process, and others rough out ideas first with image research and then afterwards refine with drawings. Reid Bartelme described how he and his partner Harriet Jung sometimes do what they term "feeling drawings," an exercise they learned in fashion school. Bartelme explained how in fashion design, they were taught to "first and foremost consider the silhouette and the feeling of it—very loose feeling sketches that didn't represent clothing but a shape, a quality of the pencil on the paper. Often just a stroke, not even on a body. This can lead to shapes of clothing or fabrications." Since they work as co-designers, the technique is helpful for them to communicate initial ideas to each other, but they prefer not to show these rough sketches to a choreographer. They do not feel the communication would translate beyond their studio.

While not her usual method, for a piece with Dwight Rhoden for San Francisco Ballet, Christine Darch's inspiration came from drawing in the rehearsal studio. She roughly sketched the dancers as they worked, and then looked at her drawing and "thought 'what is this?' And the technique came from the style of the line in the drawing. What I drew in the studio was the rendering that we used." From the gesture in her drawing, she figured out a stitching technique that wound over the surface of the costumes. The performance venue is quite large, and so she worked to translate her idea into something that would be interesting to audience members in both the front rows and the balcony. "A sheer piece of metallic mesh, stitched every ¼ inch, made wavy lines and sculpted body shapes into the waves . . . even though it was a form-fitting costume, it would change with partnering, and be more or less sparkly as the dancers moved."

Looking at Fabrics or Materials

While some designers start with shape or color, many times inspiration can come from fabrics. Looking at materials can inspire thoughts of textures and patterns—an iridescent shimmer, a bark-like roughness, a bold geometric graphic. A trip to the fabric store can also help to see if the fabric will float or ripple as it moves through space. Will it hug the form or sculpt it?

Branimira Ivanova—*Silent Ghost* by Alejandro Cerrudo at Santa Fe Ballet (Premiere 2015)

As she began her design for *Silent Ghost*, Branimira Ivanova came across some linen stretch fabric. At first, she was not sure why the yardage caught her fancy, and then she realized that she wanted linen specifically because it wrinkles. The piece was a fluid work of contemporary ballet by Alejandro Cerrudo, set to subtle music and ambient sound. She wanted the costumes to change gradually over the course of the dance, and linen would be able to achieve this for her. "When the dancers start the piece, they are perfectly pressed. By the end they are wrinkled. And the wrinkles reflect the light differently—all of a sudden it becomes used." She kept the silhouette simple and body skimming, but both the men's and women's outfits had a bit of drape to them. The fabric was the perfect weight—not too heavy but not gauzy. The palette, in subtle cool grays, went well with the shadowy lighting.

Developing Prototypes

Prototypes, sample versions of a costume, play a role for most designers during their process. While for some it comes later, after they have developed detailed ideas and drawn sketches, others like to work out ideas directly in three dimensions with fabric. Designers may play with a length of fabric on a dress form, seeing how it drapes and folds, or they may actually pattern and sew garments to try out shapes. Many designers who work this way prefer to have their own shop or studio where they can build costumes, or at least the prototype version. Mary Jo Mecca requires an apartment with an extra room—a perfect shop space—so she can work on any timeline. "If I find myself having a major pulse of energy in the middle of the night, I want to be able to go to a separate room where I've left it, and get to it."

Designer Liz Vandal sketches when she creates story ballets, but she prefers to go right to prototypes for modern dance. She has her own fabrication studio, so she can create garments or have them created on any timeline she needs. She has long-established work relationships with many choreographers, so she also feels more certain which ideas will work, and therefore is willing to risk the time and the fabric at this early stage.

When working with choreographer Marie Chouinard, one of her long-term collaborators, they chose to not discuss the costume ideas at the outset. Instead, to develop a design, Vandal would watch rehearsal and then go directly to building prototypes, which she often tested on herself before fitting the dancers. Her prototypes were often a rough draft, the equivalent of a quick sketch. Sometimes Vandal would just pin them together rather than sewing them. Then they could look at the samples together on the dancers, so that Chouinard could see the costume ideas in three dimensions and the designer could adjust the clothes as they talked. Vandal found that this method worked best for this particular collaborative partnership. "We had an average of at least 90 percent success the first time. That was the magic." Sometimes the designer's ideas helped to shape the choreography. Vandal found a very unique fabric that excited her—a permanent-pleated lamé organza. She played with the stiff sheer metallic fabric and developed a full body covering. She asked Chouinard if they could try it out. "We put two dancers in these beautiful cocoons where they would dance, and then when they would exit, the garment fell flat [to the floor] and disappeared, and she loved it and that's how she started her piece."

COMMUNICATION STYLES AND STRATEGIES

Throughout all of the steps in the process, effective communication between costume designer and choreographer and the rest of the creative team is vital for success. The best way to make fully informed and explored choices is to have free and comfortable modes of communication, in order to have a safe space in which to create.

Choreographers may stick with a limited range of costume options because they feel sure of the outcome—how it will look and feel to dance in them. For designers to be able to try a broader range of ideas, they need to determine how best to communicate with choreographers throughout the process. Choreographer Ray Mercer described the job of the designer as "having to go into [the choreographer's] head and complete their vision." Designers are trained to talk about line and hue, and positive vs negative space. But a nuanced discussion about hue is not useful if the designer means blueish green not yellowish green, but the choreographer thinks they mean a range from vibrant to washed out. Even looking at sample paint chips or color fields together is only productive if both can communicate why they like or dislike certain options. Perhaps talking about the feeling evoked by a color, linking colors to music, or working with fabric samples that show not only the color but the way it will move would be more productive. Improvisation is a necessary tool to figuring out good communication just as it is in other parts of the process.

Likewise, choreographers need to figure out how to talk to designers. The initial movement phrases show their intent and can convey a lot of information—movement quality, pacing, use of space. Listening to music selections shows mood and tempo. While just having the designer react to what they see and hear might be enough for some partnerships, others may fare better if designers can get a clearer idea of the goals. Most designers can understand the basics of choreography, especially if they see it, but some connect better to the dance when the choreographer brings supplemental images, text, or conversation about the back story. Costume designer Melanie Watnick understands that choreography is an abstract language, and so she feels that images, quotes or "anything that can help describe the internal world the choreographer relates to is helpful. [For the choreographer] it's like trying to describe what soup tastes like to someone who's not eating it." But when choreographers pull fashion magazine pages or draw sketches to show their ideas, they will be better served if they use them to open a conversation. Being given images of clothes can sometimes make a designer feel like their job is now merely to execute. The choreographer should explain what the image is actually selected to convey. Is it the color, the shape or the feeling of the gesture?

How Do You Talk About Ideas?

Both designers and choreographers commonly have questions or specifications that are part of an initial conversation about a piece, things that help a costume designer get a sense of the scope, shape and style of a piece. These may include the total number of dancers, a breakdown of groupings such as large groups vs solos and trios. Is there partnering, floor work or other movement that directly affects the functionality of the costumes? Is gender important in the piece or is the look more gender neutral? Are the dancers abstract beings, individual people, or characters? Is there an intended mood, style, or genre for the piece? What is the performance space like, and will there be scenery? Are there certain lighting effects that the choreographer already envisions? (For a checklist of questions to ask, see the Appendix at the end of this book.) At initial meetings, the choreographer may know all the answers to these questions, or only some of them. Depending on how a choreographer approaches their journey, they may already have planned most details of the production, or the designer's questions may spark them to picture their embryonic creation in the mind's eye and begin to see forms in detail.

While designers vary in how much initial information they want from a choreographer, most prefer some freedom to maneuver. Harriet Jung said, "I like when the choreographer has a clear idea of what the piece is about, but without visual references for us. That's the best because then we get to take their idea and we get to run with it from the costume standpoint." Her co-designer Reid Bartelme added, "If they are very clear about what they are trying to make as a choreographer and then they give us the freedom to make choices based on what we see inside of the work, that is ideal for us." In the same vein choreographer Amy Seiwert said, "When I make a piece, I don't want to say exactly what the costumes are. I want to give my ideas to them and then to have someone else give their ideas back. And hopefully, their ideas might spark a new idea for me and then I might say something that would spark a new idea for them."

Communication between collaborators is always smoother when the artists have an established history and know each other's working styles. Many artists stress the importance of not only having a prior work relationship but also having a personal rapport. Choreographer Trey McIntyre explained how he learned this from costume designer Sandra Woodall. "We spend a lot of time *not* talking about the piece, which is really helpful . . . What is going on with you? What are the themes in your life that you will be tearing open? Because those things are going to inform [the work]."

How Do You Communicate Visually?

Choreographers have several ways to communicate visually with collaborators. They can show their actual work in progress, perhaps finished choreography of a section or some movement phrases. Many also like to show images, and some even draw their own. The images might be suggestions for the actual appearance of the costumes, the lighting, the scenery, or broader inspirational images that show feelings or ideas metaphorically. The choreographer may have a very concrete reason for showing an image, or it might be something that speaks to them at a gut level.

Costume designers communicate visually with research images, fabric samples, sketches and prototypes. Both designers and choreographers often compile collections of digital images, or text or email images back and forth in a dialog. Choreographer Amy Seiwert finds visual references key to communicating with designers. "Sharing images is really handy. I work in a non-narrative form so if I can show images that tends to be really helpful." Ana Maria Alvarez collects images as she puts together ideas for a new work, prior to even involving designers in the process. "I do a Pinterest page of things that resonate with me: the feeling, the vibration, the colors, also videos, but not the literal look." Nicole Haskins described a meeting with costume designer Susan Roemer: "She had a bunch of sketches and fabric swatches. So many options and they were all amazing. And in what she did I saw things that I had never imagined but had been my intention. And in that coffee meeting we went through them and came up with something that was none of those designs, but all of those designs."

While many kinds of visual reference can be helpful in initial conversations, designer Christine Darch does not like when choreographers look at her past designs on her website for ideas of a look they want. "The way I design is for one person—my work looks totally different for another. I try to support what

[the choreographer is] doing when they create a dance, so of course it would be very different."

Some choreographers like to leave the details to the costume designer, while others like to be intimately involved in the decision-making. *The Gettin'* is a work by Kyle Abraham responding to the struggle in South Africa in the 1960s, set to the music of Max Roach's 1960 jazz composition *Freedom Now Suite*. Designer Karen Young researched clothing of the time. She and Abraham went through it and once they decided the overall look had the right feeling, they talked about details of fabric and silhouette. Abraham was impressed with how Young went "a little bit beyond" in her detail-oriented work on the piece. Rather than just showing the choreographer fabric samples that she collected, they decided to go to stores together, so he would be able to really experience the look and feel of the fabric options. Abraham recalled how she explained to him why different fabrics could or couldn't work. "Looking at colors and fabrics together was really exciting and important."

Sketches are standard tools for communicating design ideas, and they are much easier to change than built garments. But designers know that many choreographers do not really get a good sense of the look of a garment from a sketch, and so they move quite early into prototype ideas to continue the conversation. Looking at a costume together, on a dancer's body, allows both artists to be very clear with each other about what is working and what needs to change. They can see how the fabric flows, whether the shape flatters the dancer's body, and whether the costume hinders any of the movement. That way they can be sure the design is heading in the right direction before all the costumes are built, and with ample time to make changes prior to dress rehearsal.

Years into their working relationship, costume designer Liz Vandal wanted to try a different style with choreographer Marie Chouinard. However, because she knew her collaborator so well, she also knew it might not be well-received. As showing prototypes was their usual way of communicating, she made samples of her new idea. "I did these very 40s-type undergarments in silk satin, very sexy clothing. I wanted to see her dancers in *clothing*. I had had enough of these very organic . . . insects . . . I showed her these guys in tuxedos, and they were so sexy, and she freaked out completely." However, Vandal also knew how to keep her collaborator happy, and reassured her that this new look was just an experiment. "She said, 'how can you do that to me?' I said, 'I didn't do that to you, I am exploring things. If you don't like it, no problem, I can bring in another set of costumes tomorrow.' Because I had prepared a second set. I wanted to see it for myself, to see if she was open to go in that direction. I showed her the second version and she loved it, but it was similar to what we usually did."

Including Dancers in the Conversation

Choreographers vary in how much dancer input they want in their pieces. Some treat the dancers as co-choreographers or make the dancer's personality or personal history a feature of the work. Others see the dancers as vital, but as executors, not creators. However, most choreographers and designers want dancers to be comfortable while performing so that they can concentrate on the performance. "These are athletes. They are going to put on their skin suit to win the race. They should feel like they could bring home the gold," stated Liz Gerring. Suiting the costume to specific dancers can be something that happens in the initial conceptualization phase—their bodies or personalities can be the actual inspiration for the costume or the choreography. Or, after the initial concept is in place, costume details might be adjusted to suit each design to the wearer.

A dancer's comfort can be just about how the costume feels and whether it restricts them, or it can mean giving them a say on the aesthetics, to ensure they feel empowered. Costume designer Elena Comendador, a former dancer herself, wants to be sure the dancers have some input on how the lines of the costume cut their bodies. She feels that each dancer is an expert on his or her own body. On one dancer, a sleeve that sits just below the elbow might lengthen the arm in a flattering way, whereas on another, it might cut the arm too much in half, and a shorter or longer sleeve would work better. When fitting Misty Copeland in a capri-length unitard, Comendador recalled that "Misty stood in front of the mirror . . . moving her legs to figure out where she wanted it (the hem). She has the most beautiful calves and they are hard to figure out in terms of proportion—they sit closer to the knee than many others.'"

When and What to Ask for and About

When the choreographer asks for a specific look, designers need to determine whether that is really what they want, or just them trying to present a possible solution. Designer Emily Morgan noted that younger choreographers are often used to having to do everything on their own, as they may not have worked in venues that gave them designers to support their vision. They come in with very specific ideas, and she has learned how to "peel back the layers to figure out what the piece would actually look like in their secret heart if they had all the resources in the world." She tries to get them to not worry about what can be done and trust her to figure something out. "Instead, tell me what your dream is," she suggests, "and I'll tell you about what is possible."

Choreographer Christopher K. Morgan learned "that as long as there is time or resources, then it's OK to ask for changes, and things can keep evolving. At points [during my career] I was hesitant to speak up, and then was unsatisfied at the end. You can be surprised how late in the process people can make changes." Of course, to be a good collaborator, he also had to learn how to ask. Most designers want to be sure that the piece is as good as it can be, and that the dance truly achieves the vision of its creator. When working on a piece with the author, Morgan had a late-breaking idea just before dress rehearsal to add a moment into the dance when a dancer would stand on a chair, and then a skirt would appear "out of nowhere" and cover her legs and the chair. Crucially, Morgan asked respectfully, and explained his reasons for the request. And I, the designer, could see that he was genuinely excited about it. Additionally, in this case the new idea was actually not that hard to implement. Morgan could not have known that I had ages ago built a burlesque dress for a musical that did a similar trick, and so I had a head start on how to make it happen.

Once designers and choreographers have developed a solid foundation and ensured that they are heading in a mutually agreeable direction, they can evolve their ideas and refine them into something ready for the stage. With the various forms of dialog, the timing and the true intent of the communication can be as important as the content. Designer Elena Comendador always wants to be sure that she is inserted into the process, which helps her motivation for the project and ensures she is not left out of any key changes or ideas. "I prefer to be in there when they are all working on it. I feel like I'm in that same pool where everybody's trying to figure out what they are doing, so I don't feel so isolated and lonely about my thing over here. I don't want to be left out. I want to be part of it."

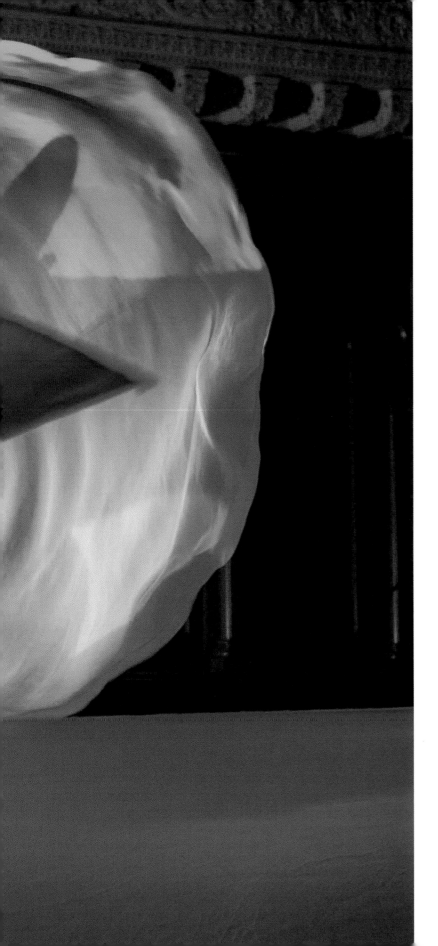

Case Study #5

Ice Cycle and *Wind Rose*

CHOREOGRAPHER—JODY SPERLING

COMPANY—TIME LAPSE DANCE

PREMIERE DATE OF *ICE CYCLE*—2015

PREMIERE DATE OF *WIND ROSE*—2019

DATE PHOTOGRAPHED—APRIL 2019

**PERFORMANCE VENUE—THE CENTER AT WEST
PARK IN NEW YORK, NY**

MUSIC—MATTHEW BURTNER

COSTUME DESIGN—MARY JO MECCA

LIGHTING DESIGN—DAVID FERRI

DRAMATURGE FOR *ICE CYCLE*—PELE BAUSCH

**PROJECTION DESIGN FOR *ICE CYCLE*—
MATTHEW HABER AND CHELSIE MCPHILIMY**

**(NOTE—NO PROJECTIONS WERE USED IN THE
PERFORMANCE PHOTOGRAPHED)**

Dancer Jenny Campbell performs in *Ice Cycle*

Dancer Alex Bittner performs in *Ice Cycle*

Jody Sperling's choreography takes inspiration from modern dance pioneer Loie Fuller. "My dance company is called Time Lapse Dance," said Artistic Director Jody Sperling. "What a time lapse does is reveal the shape of change. You see a building going up, or a flower blooming—you can't see the movement. You don't see what is between. The time lapse reveals that change. I had always thought of this [as a] connection with Loie Fuller."

Fuller, who worked in the late nineteenth and early twentieth century, evolved from burlesque skirt-dancing into a more sophisticated art, using ever-larger billowing circles of silk. To enable greater precision of movement with the fabric, she added rods to extend the reach of her arms, which gave the swirling skirts a wing-like appearance. In addition to creating a new mode of choreography, she was also an innovator who developed lighting effects and projections to use in her performances. Sperling, continuing this method, uses voluminous ponchos of silk that the dancers manipulate with wands into swirling vortexes and flower-like shapes. As a result of working for many years in this style, Sperling has become an expert at figuring out what features a costume needs to enable the choreography she envisions for each piece.

She collaborates with costume designers and makers to vary the circular costumes to suit the needs of each work. "There are so many possibilities for proportion, fabric, etc. Each [detail] has such ramifications for movement possibilities: where it's gathered, how it's gathered, those have effect." For Sperling, the costume becomes an extension of the dancer's body, and so she refers to the garment as an apparatus, as much a prosthetic as a covering. "It's costuming but it enables a whole new vocabulary." She creates pieces for both solo dancers and groups that feature swirling fabric, skillfully manipulated into gradually undulating twirling shapes. "The main idea is it extends your body and allows you to create these enduring trace forms." Physics are always on her mind. Each change of angle or speed must be calibrated so the fabric can keep its momentum and not get tangled or piled up. Heavier fabric moves differently than lighter weight, and while the outer edge of the poncho or cape is always voluminous, variations in fullness affect the range of motion and the fabric's behavior. Dancers learn to move the apparatus in cannon or in unison, filling the space with flutter and wind.

Sperling is an internationally known expert on Loie Fuller, and she was selected to choreograph the French movie *La Danseuse*, which premiered at the 2016 Cannes Film Festival. For this movie about Fuller, Sperling spent five weeks teaching the actor to perform the dances. But in addition to her dance duties, she also had to work with the costume team to show them what was needed. Originally, they thought they could just make something that looked like the photos of Fuller. Sperling had to explain to them how important nuances of cut and shape were, to be sure the costume could actually create the choreography needed. Sperling earned a 2017 World Choreography Award nomination for her work on the film.

COSTUMES

Clearly, for Sperling's work to be successful, she needs to collaborate very closely with a costume designer. She has worked with several over the course of her career, and her current collaborator is Mary Jo Mecca. They work together well, and the two of them also collaborate frequently with costume painter Gina Nagy Burns. Sperling describes the effortless give and take of a good collaboration. "Once you do all the homework there is an intuition flow you get into."

When she first saw the work of Time Lapse Dance, the costumes piqued Mary Jo Mecca's curiosity. She thought, "Oh my god these are phenomenal! How are they constructed?" She agreed to work with Sperling because of the challenge. It was a different kind of work than she had done before. Mecca recalls her first discussions with Sperling. "What is fascinating about Jody is she is so intelligent. She was talking about mathematical formulas of circumference, how many pounds, etc. What is needed to make this shape or that shape? We spent a great deal of time dissecting one of her pieces, just measuring. A lot of measuring." The capes need to be calibrated precisely for each dancer. And of course, there are yards and yards of silk panels to join together and hem. "It's very labor intensive. You can't mass produce them and have them look as great as hers."

Mary Jo Mecca began her career in the arts as an actor. She was looking for a more hands-on creative outlet and stumbled upon the Alice Sapho School of Dressmaking and Design near her home on the Upper West Side of Manhattan. "The greatest thing [Sapho] taught me was she unlocked my mechanical eye, my dissecting eye." After completing her studies in fashion construction and design, she was asked to design a piece for a modern dance company. Mecca used her experience gleaned during her time as a performer to combine her fashion skills with costume design. "I started to dissect [dance] the way I would dissect a script. I have always been a performer that would sit out and watch to see what the big picture was." She

Jody Sperling performing in Ice Cycle

Carly Cerasuolo and Sperling

Nyemah Stuart, Morgan Bontz & Carly Cerasuolo in *Ice Cycle*

"started to look at dance for what was required—was there knee work, partner work, repetition?"

While Mecca also works with other choreographers whose work gives her freer rein for her designs, she enjoys the technical challenge of working with someone who is such a specialist. "Jody has very strong ideas of why and what she wants, and I facilitate that for her. Mathematically what she has figured out, I can make that happen." She enjoys the problem-solving needed to create the right shapes and finessing the details of construction. Mecca recalls wanting to be secure and comfortable in her costume when she used to dance. "I wanted to feel like I was built for war." And she wants that for the Time Lapse dancers as well.

ICE CYCLE

Ice Cycle was inspired by Sperling's real-life research in the Arctic, observing and dancing on sea ice. She was invited to be part of a 2014 expedition on the US Coast Guard Cutter Healy, one of several non-scientists on the trip. Sperling is a passionate advocate for stopping climate change and for the plight of sea ice, which is disappearing at an alarming rate. She wanted to find a way to bring the Arctic directly to audiences and help them relate the effects of global warming to local climate change issues.

Sperling based some of her choreography for *Ice Cycle* quite literally on the science of sea ice. At the beginning of the piece, one dancer has a long piece of white silk wrapped around her body. She begins to unwind with a glacial slowness, pulling against another dancer who holds the end of the silk. As she progresses across the stage, the fabric forms a wall upon which images of sea ice are projected, accompanied by the sound of dripping water. The dancer unwinds gradually faster, echoing the rapid progression of the melting ice seen in the footage. "The next section is based on crystal formation. Everything is in a spoke formation. I was literally thinking about two hydrogens and an oxygen," the molecular structure of ice. A section with a duet between one dancer in a white cape and one in black, representing ice and water, is about the Albedo ratio, which is a measure of how reflective or absorbent of light a surface is, the ratio of reflected light to incident light. "I was interested in this idea of the ice and the water," Sperling said. "In the past there was a balance between [them]. Even when it's all frozen there are cracks where there is open water. Using an intricate rhythm in a six-count meter, the dancers entwine and wrap around each other like a yin and yang."

One dancer in a black unitard rises up from behind the translucent wall of stretched silk like an incoming tide. She used movement Sperling generated when she danced on icebergs in the Arctic. The dancer's outstretched arms define the horizon. After a time, she reaches over the wall, breaking the plane and delineating the space. Next, in a contrasting section, a dancer in a large white cape swirls in and out of the space above the wall, her reach so much taller and broader than human arms.

"[Sperling] knows what that cape is capable of doing, and she is always finding new and interesting things," Mecca explains. When Sperling wanted to add choreography that wasn't hidden by the apparatus, the designer helped her develop an "uncluttered" look that would function well for the dance. The dancers needed to change quickly in and out of the cape during the dance, so they decided that a streamlined unitard was the best choice to function well under the voluminous silk. Mecca chose to do a racer-back style to make the arms look longer, accentuating their natural form, since in the rest of the dance they are completely hidden. The mock-turtleneck shape echoes the insulated unitard Mecca created for Sperling when she danced in the Arctic and works well with the gathered high neckline of the silk capes.

The costume variations show the cycle of ice and water throughout the piece. White is the fully formed ice, while the pale gray is the newer ice, and black is the water. Each dancer has a cape that matches the color of the unitard they wear beneath. For the choreographer, the structure and substance of the capes represent ice, while the "naked" body in just a unitard represents water. At the end of the piece, the dancers appear in translucent gray chiffon capelets over their unitards, much smaller garments that only partially cover the dancer. They are translucent and float around the dancer. Sperling explained "When we see the dancers in the end with the capelets, they are water returning, the melting of ice into water." She closed the piece with these capelets instead of the large silk apparatus because "I did want the audience to feel something was missing at the end." Mecca made the sleeveless capelets open in the front, so while the dancers are partially sheathed in the misty gray chiffon, their true forms show strongly beneath.

Maki Kitahara in the horizon solo from *Ice Cycle*, composer Matthew Burtner is in the background.

Dancers of Time Lapse Dance in *Wind Rose* using sticks in the capes

WIND ROSE

Wind Rose explores the patterns of wind. While a dancer usually moves through the air without the air itself being noticeable, the diaphanous costumes of Time Lapse Dance let the audience actually see and even feel the air. A wind rose is a meteorological method used to graph wind speed and direction, and the dancers in *Wind Rose* perform a similar function. They chart the ripples and gusts coming from their own velocity as they swirl the costumes up, down and around. "One of the central problems with climate change is that we haven't been noticing that it's happening because we *literally* live in climate-controlled environments," Sperling explains. "I believe it's important to start noticing the air as it moves around us—its currents, temperature, pressure—and to start to feel these changes sensorially, viscerally, so we can understand what's happening and feel the urgency of action."

Sperling developed an interest in the link between climate change and wind. She noticed more turbulent wind happening in her native New York City, and when she researched the phenomenon, she learned that while local winds were becoming more extreme

and unpredictable, global winds were actually slowing. Sperling describes how she created movement that would help the audience to see and feel these changes. "In the opening, the dancers are walking in a circle to create a turbine. This pathway is very good at creating a gush of air towards the audience. This circling is the central choreographic motif of the first section . . . I came to think of the pattern as the ongoing jet stream. At the end of this section, we simulate a polar vortex, where the jet stream becomes wonky, collapsing into wobbly sine curves, and abandoning its streamlined pattern. I wanted to have a sense of change and transformation."

Sperling had always noticed the unique sound made by the costumes when she rehearsed and decided to explore this aspect more explicitly. She first created the more playful *Sound Study* with a cellist where they used the sound of the costume as part of the music and performed a duet. She asked the composer from *Ice Cycle*, Alaskan-born environmental composer Matthew Burtner, to see if he'd be interested in collaborating on a new piece. He and Sperling share an interest in the artistic study of climate change and the Arctic, which led to their first collaboration. Since wind is heard

Dancer Nyemah Stuart in *Wind Rose*

at least as much as felt, it seemed a fitting topic to explore both visually and musically.

To accentuate the sonic possibilities of the costumes, Sperling chose to use a slightly heavier silk for the apparatuses for this piece. She developed a vocabulary of specific movements with the costumes that generated different sounds—swishes from moving the silk-covered arm through space, sharp cracks like a whip, or dull slaps when the fabric hits against the ground. She choreographed and named eight four-bar movement sequences that each had their own specific rhythm. "The Houdini is when the fabric slaps together in the front. It makes a poof then it flaps together in the back and makes a poof. Then there is the sound when you trace a table plane with your arm—it makes a whoosh." Burtner took the eight sequences

and used them to write a score for the dance. He also added a few rhythmic variations of his own. "It was for five dancers and he sent a five-part fugue. It was tricky for the dancers to learn because it's all variations on [the same] eight movements," Sperling explained. "I made the music and he choreographed it."

During the performance, Burtner arranged microphones at the front of the stage, to capture both the sounds made by the costumes and the dancers' breathing as well as their more explicit vocalizations. The costumes create enough wind that he used windsocks on the microphones, the fuzzy covers that help in windy situations. The noise from the costumes and dancers is accented by a soundscape. He plays both electronic and acoustic instruments live during performance to accompany the dancers. Burtner also used the actual

Bontz and Cerasuolo in *Ice Cycle*

Dancers of Time Lapse Dance in *Wind Rose* finale section

wind rose chart as inspiration. Sperling explains that "in my solo Matthew is playing wind rose data in direct response to my spatial pathway on stage."

For added variation during the first section of the piece, the five dancers depart from their usual Loie Fuller technique of propelling the floor length silk circles with inserted poles, and instead use just their arms. Sperling made this change to create the sounds that she wanted—when the dancers strike the silk on the ground, they create a thud of just the fabric hitting rather than a clack of poles. The top half of the capes stiffened by arms, with the lower half undulating, also gives a different, more human aspect to the first section. The fabric drapes on the dancers' arching and contracting torsos, the heavier silk more flowing than floating. In the last section the dancers add the sticks back into their capes. Their movements are similar to those used earlier, but the effect is altered. When they slap the ground, the sticks make a percussive hit. The swirling fabric folds crisply on the stick-lengthened arms, turning the dancers into pinwheels and flowers. The viewer's focus is drawn to the rippling edge of the garment; the human underneath is much less noticeable. When the dancers repeat their turbine formation from the opening, the sticks greatly alter the behavior of the fabric and the overall effect of the movement. The five dancers again walk side by side with arms held out at a low angle. The center dancer turns in place and the outermost dancer moves quite briskly, the group circling like the sweeping hand of a clock. In the section without sticks the visual is of five women in long flowing garments, only the outermost dancer's cape substantially caught by the wind. With sticks, they become much more geometric and more similar. A cone-shaped tent of fabric arches around each woman, separate from her vertical form in the middle.

During the costume change when the quintet adds sticks into their capes, Sperling dances a solo dressed austerely in a form-fitting long-sleeved black top and black gauchos using just sticks, no swirling fabric. She manipulates the sticks in a similar fashion to the caped dancers, holding them as long extensions of her arm and tracing forms in the air. The sticks whipping through the air make a distinctive whistling sound effect. It looks almost like an X-ray of the previous dance. Like a ghosting after-image, she fades to the wings, and is replaced by gently rippling white columns as the group of dancers re-enter.

Stuart and Bontz in *Wind Rose* dancing without sticks in the capes

Time Lapse Dancers perform in *Ice Cycle*

5

The Process— Explorations: From Concept to Production

Once the foundations are in place, both choreographers and designers need to refine their ideas and shape them into a finished product. Depending on the artist and how they start their process, some steps listed in Chapter 4 might come into play in this stage, or vice versa. Choreographers who start with concept might add real music here while those who begin with music might discover a theme or narrative as the work takes shape. Designers who first explore their emotional response to music might choose colors and fabrics in the initial phase, but develop shapes later, after they see more of the actual movement. Designers who draw during rehearsal and start with clothing shapes might choose colors only after they hear music or see groupings of dancers as the work progresses.

This exploration stage is also usually the best time to really evaluate which ideas are workable—both in terms of realizing the vision, and in terms of logistics and constraints. Starting with logistics can hamper the creative process but waiting too long can lead to dead ends that are not good choices for the actual project.

LOGISTICS AND OUTSIDE INFLUENCES

Budget and Resources: Time, Money, Skills, Technology

Clearly any plans for costumes need to be in line with the budget and resources. Things to consider include the actual funds available

Dancers from Nashville Ballet perform Paul Vasterling's *The Four Seasons*. Costume design by David Heuvel, lighting design by Scott Leathers.

Dancers Kayla Rowser and Judson Veach in *The Four Seasons.* The Nashville Symphony is visible in the background.

Dancers Brett Sjoblom and Nicolas Scheuer from Nashville Ballet perform *The Four Seasons*.

Dancers Logan Hillman and Owen Thorne

to purchase materials or clothing and the amount of labor at hand to implement the costumes. With labor, the skillset and available technologies are as important as the quantity. What level of patterning ability does the shop have? Are there facilities for dyeing fabric, custom painting or constructing masks? The timing of the labor can also affect what is possible. How do the weeks slotted for the build compare to when the rehearsals and performances are? Can the shop make prototypes ahead of time, and also make last-minute changes during dress rehearsals? When will the dancers be available for fittings compared with when the costume-makers are available? How many costumes are actually needed—does the budget have to include spares due to understudies or double casting?

Some choreographers interviewed mentioned that they had learned to stop making assumptions about whether a given idea would be cheap or expensive, difficult or easy. Instead, they realized they should let the designers make the call about the feasibility of given ideas. A very simple-seeming costume, a basic pair of pants or a sleeveless tank dress, while not taking a lot of fabric nor being time-consuming to sew, can be expensive in materials. The fabric that achieves the right drape and color might be quite expensive or a custom dye job. Or the nuances of the shape might involve multiple prototypes until the lines hit the dancer just right both standing and leaping. Sometimes $500 can be enough, other times $5,000 can be constraining. If costumes need a watercolor hand-painted effect, that could involve hiring a professional fabric painter. There might be someone already on staff with the requisite skills. Or the designer might be lucky enough to find fabric that already has the right look.

Some choreographers mentioned that once something had been built for a lot of money, they felt like they had to keep it, whether they were happy with the look of the costume or not. And so, unless they were working with the handful of dance companies that have deep pockets, having more money invested in a project can actually make an artist feel more constrained. With a less involved costume, more change might have been possible.

While the job of costume designer and costume-maker are separate, some designers like to be in charge of both aspects of the process. Having one's own workshop lets a designer figure out ideas in three dimensions on a dress form, start prototypes whenever they are needed, and generally be more in control of the timeline of the build process. Designers Reid Bartelme and Harriet Jung usually build their own designs, and Liz Vandal had her own shop, run by a business partner, for the majority of her career.

Paul Vasterling—*The Four Seasons* for Oregon Ballet Theatre (Premiere 1997)

The resources of a dance company can even influence the actual choreographic structure of a piece. While working as a guest choreographer during the earlier part of his career, Paul Vasterling wanted to find a new angle on Vivaldi's *The Four Seasons* and decided to explore different gender groupings. "The question that I asked myself was: how are women with women? How are women with men? . . . How does that change the gender behavior?" His rehearsal period overlapped with another choreographer at the company who had seniority, which kept him from rehearsing with his entire cast at once. "I asked for as many people as I could get, which was three people—down the hall in this tiny closet. And so, I decided to do it in sections with three people, because then I could get the rehearsal time that I needed." He realized that this solution actually led him to a dance he was quite happy with. He created opening and closing sections using the whole group, and then each season was portrayed by a different trio of dancers.

Performance Space, Performance Schedule

For the overall creation of a piece, the logistics of the performance space can influence the work in both major and minor ways. The choreographer may suit the piece to the performance venue or choose a venue whose layout fits the needs of the dance. If hired to create a work for an arena space, the choreographer will make a dance that looks interesting from all sides. Or, the choreographer might conceive a work where the dancers move fluidly between the stage and the audience, and then seek out a venue that has multiple paths from stage to house. The size of the venue affects whether the audience sees small details like nuances of movement and facial expressions, and also subtleties of costume. The placement of the audience also influences a work—in a proscenium theater, the audience all sees the dance from the same angle. Thrust spaces put the audience in an arc, seeing the dance from the side as well as the front. Some spaces, arena or black-boxes, have the audience on all sides. Raked spaces allow the audience to look down on the dance, viewing more of the floor and always seeing the dancer's whole body. Other spaces have a house with minimal rake or a flat floor, which means both that they may not see floorwork well, and that they may not see lower body costume details like shoes. Dance also performs in less typical spaces, whether a converted church where the organ and stained-glass create a built-in backdrop, or a rough platform outdoors encircled by forest and lit by natural light. Both choreographers and costume designers should plan for the entire stage picture and make choices that align with the way the audience will view the work. For tours, it's a good idea to plan costumes and dances that can work in a variety of venues, with a variety of lighting setups.

The size and shape of the performance space may determine how many dancers can be in a work, where they can enter and exit, or whether a costume change can happen out of view of the audience. If dancers are performing a piece as part of an evening of works, the show order will govern whether complicated makeup is possible, or costumes that take time to put on. The performance venue also may limit what kinds of lighting, sound, projection and other technologies are possible, both in terms of what is owned and installed, and what can be added. These influence the set and lighting design, which in turn affect a choreographer's overall choices about a piece.

The performance schedule of a piece also can affect costumes— depending on how long the piece will run, durability becomes more of an issue, both with strength of the fabric itself, and how well dyes or decorations last. How frequently a piece is performed might necessitate choosing materials that can be easily laundered and dried. If a piece will tour, especially if there isn't much funding for wardrobe staff, designers should choose strong, easy-care materials that won't need a lot of maintenance like repairs or steaming. For longer runs or likely revivals and remounts, designers should design costumes that can easily be worn by more than one individual. If budget allows making new costumes for different cast members, designers must buy extra fabric at the outset, or pick something easy to source again.

Charlese Antoinette—*joyUS justUS* by Ana Maria Alvarez for Contra-Tiempo (Premiere 2018)

Costume designer Charlese Antoinette faced an unusual challenge as she prepared her design for Ana Maria Alvarez' *joyUS justUS*. The piece, a melding of contemporary dance with salsa, Cuban dance and hip hop, is about the practice of radical joy (for more detail, see Case Study #1). The company, Contra-Tiempo, was slated to tour over the course of a year. Between when the piece was initially workshopped, and the premiere performance, Antoinette learned that one of the dancers was expecting. Celebrating the heritage of each dancer was central to the development of both the choreography and the costumes—who they are as individuals as well as who they become as a community. The dancer, Isis Avalos, is Mexican American and she and the designer decided to put a suggestion of Frida Kahlo into the design, with a flower crown. Antoinette

reconceived the satin pants for the original outfit into a jumpsuit, so that the bottoms were supported from the shoulders, rather than needing anything tight at the waist. In her new version, the dancer wore slim fitted stretch shorts, covered by a semi-sheer pleated garment in the same deep green, like a skirt but open in the front. The design suggested long flowing pants but was more adaptable. The sparkling top, flower crown and woven shawl from the original design stayed unchanged.

Producers and Producing Organizations

The actual producer of a piece or performance usually has specific expectations for the works created under their umbrella. For purposes of this discussion, a producer means whoever hires the choreographer and commissions the work, whether it's a dance company hiring a guest choreographer, an artistic director to a resident choreographer, or a venue or festival hiring a dance company.

A dance company might have a specific aesthetic they prefer. This could encompass a style of choreography, genre of music, or the visual look of the dancers—costume, or even hairstyles and footwear. Companies and venues often market themselves to a particular demographic, and therefore while they want to present variety, many don't want to alienate their audiences or present works they won't enjoy. Or they want to have a specific "brand" to keep their product distinctive. Some producers might not want loud, jarring music. Some might not want too much nudity, or work that is too political. Some producers explicitly want to highlight ethnic and cultural variety. Others want work that appears "edgy" and would reject anything too traditional. According to costume designer Reid Bartelme, "Even if a ballet company is doing a more modern kind of piece, often the attitude and the culture towards costume is still a little more conservative . . . Ballet companies do have a narrower spectrum of interests in terms of silhouette and gender conformity."

Producers also have a responsibility to plan their overall seasons and to do marketing to sell tickets and woo donors. This often affects the timeline—to plan an overall season, some may need a general idea of a new piece's content or theme, both to plan an evening that flows well and has the requisite variety, and also to do marketing of the season. Sometimes a choreographer has to come up with the title for a piece prior to actually thinking in depth about the content. A company's timeline can also affect the overall design process, as costume designs might be due by a certain date for the shop to make them, even if it is before the rehearsal is underway.

Dancers from Dayton Contemporary Dance Company in *Beyond a Cliff* by Dwight Rhoden, costume and set design by L'Amour, lighting design by John Rensel.

Dancers from Dayton Contemporary Dance Company in *Beyond a Cliff*

Dancers Michael Green and Quentin ApolloVaughn Sledge

L'Amour and Dwight Rhoden—*Beyond a Cliff* for Dayton Contemporary Dance Company (Premiere 1991)

Artists working with a specific company should have the expectations in mind, although often a conversation urging them to consider a change of pace can be quite productive. In the early 1990s L'Amour designed costumes for a piece by Dwight Rhoden for Dayton Contemporary Dance called *Beyond a Cliff*. Rhoden recalled that he based the work on a poem he wrote with the same name. "It dealt with the ideas of being on the edge and how to deal with a high level of emotion . . . It also dealt with extremes." The vision that came to L'Amour as he watched the choreography was bands of white fabric crisscrossing the dancers' bodies, leaving lots of flesh exposed. The designer recalled that he and Rhoden discussed "being on the edge, indecisiveness. We talked about things we went through as friends. [This led to the] thought of on the verge of a nervous breakdown, and straitjackets." Rhoden liked the idea, but the designer knew he should also check with Jeraldyne Blunden, the founder and director of the company. L'Amour had been associated with DCDC for years, first as a dancer and then in wardrobe, so he knew that these designs would be outside of the company's comfort zone. Blunden grudgingly allowed the costumes. L'Amour realized later that they had clearly grown on her, evidenced by the fact that a photo of them was used as the central image in the company's marketing for their next international tour.

Cultural Values

Cultural values of a dance company or producer can also have a large or small influence on a work. Some companies cast dancers in all shapes and sizes. Others strive for sustainability. Some works might have to be tailored to be compatible with an audience's cultural background or religion. That might entail ensuring content would not be offensive, or just choosing themes for a work that are universal enough to resonate with international audiences during a tour.

Ray Mercer—*Through the Gate of Tears* for Smithsonian National Museum of African Art (Premiere 2014)

Choreographer Ray Mercer was commissioned to do a ballet about the country of Oman. He created a modern story ballet using African and Arabian music that told the story of an Omani man's journey from Oman to East Africa, titled *Through the Gate of Tears*. The Smithsonian's National Museum of African Art initiated the project

as part of a series, "Connecting the Gems of the Indian Ocean: From Oman to East Africa," formed to highlight cross-cultural connections, endowed by a gift from the Sultanate of Oman. Howard University produced the work in 2014, using students and faculty as well as professional dancers and designers. The project was documented in the film *Through the Gate of Tears: Backstage*.

Mercer and his collaborators researched both Oman and East Africa in order to be true to the cultures' beliefs and clothing. For the work to align with practices of Islam, he reworked his choreographic ideas so that while there might be partnering between men and women, they did not ever touch. The dancers dressed in costumes true to the silhouette and traditions of the region. Bodies were completely covered, and the women wore pants beneath their skirts to not reveal the legs when they twirled and kicked. Both men and women wore long sleeves, and the designer used long tunics for many of the dancers, although slit at the sides for movement. The women's heads were covered by hijabs and the men wore turbans. The costume designer Timm Burrow sought to be as authentic as possible although he did make some adaptations to the clothing shapes for movement. He used as many fabrics from the actual cultures as budget and logistics allowed.

The project was a challenge for the choreographer, and a new experience for the dancers. Mercer worked with the cast to do bigger movements that would translate through the costumes. While originally it felt like a restriction to not see the body as he was used to, he grew to like this look. He saw how the fabric moved with the dancers and the layers accentuated the movement. Burrow designed shapes that were suitable but fluid, and Mercer stated that he never had to adjust his movements for the costumes. The restrictions gave a new stimulus to his creativity, and the piece is one he cited as one of his proudest accomplishments.

Robin Shane—*Waves of Plastic* by Laney Engelhard with Artichoke Dance and Rider University (Premiere 2019)

Sustainability is a value many arts organizations including dance companies are working to incorporate. Whether reusing materials, choosing ecologically responsible practices, or purchasing responsibly sourced items, arts organizations are looking into ways to help the planet. Rider University partnered with Artichoke Dance Company and with other environmental groups for a sustainability-themed dance concert. Artichoke Dance, founded by Lynn Neuman, has a mission to promote environmental consciousness through both performances and education. For the dance concert, the mission was not only to use sustainable materials and practices, but also for each dance to have a theme that related to the environment. Each of the six works was created by a different choreographer and had its own point of view.

Robin Shane, the costume designer for the concert, used either recycled or sustainable materials for all of the costumes, spending no money. "The challenge is to use these types of materials but still focus first on the actual design, the needs of the piece . . . and to use different materials for each piece." The designer realized that although the logistics were more overt with this project, the balance between external factors and art was the same one she always has to navigate when designing. She had to consider what the piece is about and the shape she wanted her design to take, while simultaneously keeping in mind the short time allotted for the build. "How do you balance all of those things and make something that works, tells the story, and is beautiful?" she asked.

Shane felt that her most successful collaboration in the concert was *Waves of Plastic* with Laney Engelhard, because "the choreographer really incorporated the skirts into the piece." It was one of the few works where if she asked herself the question "would this be something I would choose to do if the theme were not sustainability?" the answer would be yes. The initial conversation with Engelhard, over email, told her that the work would be contemporary ballet, and "she used words like *swooshy*." She told Shane that she wanted the dancers' costumes to evoke the ocean, and that she was thinking of blue skirts, possibly with an ombre, and would love for the skirts to be made of plastic bags. Shane replied that while the choreographer's suggestion of spray paint would not work well with the thin plastic, she would look into dyeing or other ways to vary the color and asked her questions about skirt shape. They determined that the skirts should evoke a romantic tutu.

Shane did some sketches, and then tried tests with the materials. She took large translucent white and transparent blue trash bags from the custodians' stockpile at the university and played with different ways to use the plastic to create layers and color variation in the skirts. She sent the choreographer images of four versions: one was of even rectangular strips, gradating in length and color, that mimicked the volume of a romantic tutu. One was gradually shorter full skirts one on top of the next, shifting from blue to white. Shane tried fusing bags with heat into larger sheets, and then cut and sewed a stiff A-line skirt. And she made a skirt of torn irregular pieces that intermixed both colors. "What was great about the plastic is the way it kind of stretches as you tear it," Shane said, which gave the edges texture. Both designer and choreographer liked the torn version best.

Shane also sent the choreographer videos to show her how the different versions moved. Shane recalled that she was pleased with the way the strips of plastic moved but was afraid the noise they made could be a problem. But the choreographer loved the sound, and thought it sounded like water. Shane didn't realize the full plan until she saw a run of the work later. "At some point she cut the music, so it was silent, and had the dancers brushing their hands across the plastic. It made a 'swish, swish' sound that sounded like the ocean . . . [The choreographer] understood what the material could do, and how it could add to the auditory experience of the piece." The completed costumes were the skirts of plastic strips, with some bits of gray bags added in for additional texture, worn over leotards pulled from stock. Shane and her shop decorated the leotards with dimensional appliqués that evoked seaweed or coral, also made from plastic bags. Overall Shane was pleased with how the costumes worked with the overall dance to "tell the story in more than just a visual way. It was magical." The skirts were so successful that Artichoke Dance adopted them to use in a different work performed in repertory by their company.

The overall concert used sustainable materials not only in the costumes, but also as scenery and props. Several of the works had sculptural pieces made of plastic waste. Additionally, the concert did not use a paper program. Instead the audience viewed a slideshow of the credits and a weblink to an online version. In place of paper tickets, the audience members received bracelets made of plastic bags. Shane explained that the audience was given the memento to further underscore the fact that plastic will never leave the planet, "something beautiful, but also a constant reminder." Going forwards, the experience inspired Shane to start a chapter of the Broadway Green Alliance at Rider University. Each show has a green captain who oversees that more sustainable practices are used in each production.

EVOLUTION DURING REHEARSAL

How do design and choreography influence each other? Even seasoned professionals cannot foresee exactly how a dance and a costume will combine. Watching the costume in motion for the first time can be exciting and can spark new ideas. It can also be a time for editing and troubleshooting.

Jenny Rocha—*Battledress* for Rocha Dance Theater (Premiere 2013)

Sometimes a costume needs to be adjusted to make the choreography work. Other times the costume might inspire a different twist in the choreography. Sometimes it's both. Choreographer and costume designer Jenny Rocha was mid-process in the creation of her piece *Battledress*, discussed in more detail in Chapter 2. As part of the work, she wanted to incorporate hoop skirts because of the limitations they would impose on the movement. She first ordered premade ones, to test the idea out. Once her dancers tried them in rehearsal, she realized it would serve the piece better to see the legs, so she made sheer ones. While interesting, the costume still was not communicating the displaced, out of joint feeling she was hoping for. "And then I had a thought during rehearsal. I flipped upside down and the dancers thought it looked really cool. So, I created a whole section of us being lost women, just walking legs with the hoop covering the top half of the body."

Adjusting Design for Choreography

Once the choreographer, costume designer and other designers have established basic ideas for the work, they ideally stay in close contact as they refine their ideas, to be sure that the ideas remain compatible. As much as possible, designers should continue to view rehearsals as they finesse their design. That way, they can watch the movement while picturing the dancers wearing the costumes. They might realize that a certain move on the floor could get the dancer's legs tangled in the panels of the skirt or realize that a flowing arm gesture would be nicer if the sleeve had more volume. Through fitting photos, looking at costumes together in the costume shop, or rehearsal with prototypes, choreographers should have plenty of chance to see the costumes as they evolve. When they see the costume taking shape, they can better understand the designer's ideas and suggest changes if desired.

Emily Morgan—*Realms of Amber* by Edgar Zendejas (Premiere 2016)

Costume designer Emily Morgan was working on *Realms of Amber* at Richmond Ballet, (profiled in more detail in Chapter 3) and a row of buttons down the back of the women's dresses that connected the design with a memory of her grandmother's wedding dress was central to her design inspiration. However, as she watched the dancers in rehearsal, she realized that for a lot of the partnering,

the men put their hands on the women's backs. Morgan was concerned that the buttons would be too uncomfortable or make the grip unstable. Since the idea was so central to her design, rather than scrapping the idea, she asked two of the male dancers who she knew were good at troubleshooting to meet with her in the costume shop. An advantage of being the resident designer for the company was she knew the dancers well. With some experimentation, they realized that if they took the metal loops off the back of the buttons, it still gave the look she wanted, but the discs were flat enough not to get in the dancers' way. Morgan had the costume shop just sew the fabric-covered discs directly to the bodice as decoration. They added flat hooks to actually hold the garment closed underneath.

Reid & Harriet Design—*Recomposed* by Doug Varone for Doug Varone and Dancers (Premiere 2015)

Reid & Harriet Design collaborated with choreographer Doug Varone on a work called *Recomposed*. The choreography was inspired by a series of abstract pastel drawings by Joan Mitchell, and so the designers studied the drawings to come up with an idea for the costumes. "We made all the dancers these black unitards, each of which had a vertical strip of a bold color, and over it they have a net suit, like a jumpsuit. The jumpsuit has dangling strips of color inside of it . . . We go in stages of exploring and we wanted to really explore color, and we were in the middle of a transparency phase," designer Reid Bartelme explained. Varone wasn't sure how he felt about the idea when he saw the sketches, but he was open to exploring with the designers. Once he tried the costumes in rehearsal, he was inspired to use the costumes two ways—with just the unitards uncovered, and also with the pale sheer jumpsuits over, as originally intended. While this was not how the designers had planned the costumes, they were happy with Varone's use of them "because the net suit kind of obscured the unitard and played with the light." Further, the two different costume looks, one bold and graphic, one a muted, softened version, gave a different character to the overall piece, creating a change in tone depending on how the dancers were dressed.

Changing Choreography for Design

As a costume design evolves, it may inspire the choreographer to make adjustments. The changes can be to ensure that the costume can function as intended, or because the look of the costumes inspires changes to the movement. Choreographer Dwight Rhoden recounted the experience of working with the flowing, sheer pants designed by Christine Darch for the work *Mercy*. The pants were so full that when the dancers stood still, they seemed to be in a skirt but when they moved it was clear they wore pants. "They were more flowy than I originally thought they would be. I think that I went even further with making sure that the movement . . . enhanced the sweeping of the [costume], a lot of the leg work became a little more circular."

Sometimes the influence of a costume on a piece is subtle, sometimes it's something central to the work. Choreographer Ray Mercer created a piece for a group of women. From the outset, he knew that he wanted a quick change in one count to be a part of the work. So, early on in the process, he met with the costume designer to be sure the idea would be possible. "The dancers hated it because it was a lot of work, but it was fun to look at. It was like a nude unitard and the dress was tucked into the bodice at the top. When they turned, they released the top part and it turned into this short red dress." They worked with a prototype and made adjustments to the skirt fabric to get it thin enough to hide, but heavy enough to fall. He also had to make adjustments to his choreography to change where and how the dancers pulled the unitard to make it release and spent significant rehearsal time to ensure all five dancers could do it in unison.

Jack Ferver—*Everything is Imaginable* for New York Live Arts (Premiere 2018)

As part of the process of creating the work *Everything is Imaginable,* choreographer Jack Ferver asked each of the five dancers to name their childhood icon off the top of their head. From this, he developed a multifaceted work about identity. Ferver enlisted his frequent collaborators, costume design team Reid Bartelme and Harriet Jung, to translate the icons into dynamic, danceable clothing. Ferver told the designers "it's these men, these queer men, playing their childhood icons. James Whiteside is *not* Judy Garland, you [Bartelme also performed in the piece] are *not* My Little Pony, I am *not* Michelle Pfeiffer in *Batman Returns.*" The costume designers created a look for each dancer based on their character, but in sheer fabric to highlight the vulnerability, as well as to show the male bodies underneath. As the piece developed, the costume design influenced Ferver in creating a section of the work.

The Judy Garland costume for dancer James Whiteside was a sparkling late 1950s tunic-dress. Once Ferver thought about the costume with the choreography for Whiteside's solo, he realized that "There was a place where he was doing a cartwheel, and that the dress would come down and you would see him in a dance belt, and we were going to start dealing with the male body and its virtuosity in this costume, and that is beautiful." This realization helped him to think through the balance between camp and the icon herself. It "helped build an addendum to the number—a tap number—that helped relate it more to Judy . . . The big loud gay person [version of] Judy could be laughed at and treated like a clown, camp like, but the tap section was small and nuanced and could lead to the rest of the show."

John Ahrens—*Carved in Stone* by Joy Bollinger for Bruce Wood Dance (Premiere 2016)

Costume designer John Ahrens recalled a transformation that happened while working on Joy Bollinger's *Carved in Stone* at Bruce Wood Dance. The costumes he designed were very full pants for the men, and long circle skirts for the women, in subtle pale gray tones. "There were ruined columns on stage, and I made the costumes to look similar. Tony [Tucci] lit it so you didn't know if they were clothed, or even if they were human, at first." The opening sequence of the choreography had the dancers standing in place, moving just their upper bodies. When they saw it in dress rehearsal, he and Bollinger realized that if the dancers bent their knees slightly, they looked even more like part of the scenery. The choreographer chose to keep this look, starting the dance with living columns on stage who then broke free and danced.

Karen Young—*Sleeping Beauty* with Alexandro Cerrudo at Theater Basel (Premiere 2016)

Karen Young designed costumes for a production of *Sleeping Beauty* at Theater Basel with choreographer Alejandro Cerrudo. The choreographer's original plan for the ballet called for Princess Aurora to float in the air, dreamlike, using a harness. Young's costume design for the Princess was a delicate chiffon dress. The choreographer really wanted the look of chiffon for the character, but Young was afraid that the fabric would not be compatible with the harness. She worried it would be too fragile and wasn't sure if it could adequately conceal the apparatus on the dancer. They tried several kinds of harnesses, but the choreographer never liked the look of her dancing in the harness, she wasn't horizontal enough to "sleep." Instead, Cerrudo found a way to suspend the dancer without the harness.

The princess laid across two supports, one under her back and one under her legs, and she didn't have to wear anything besides her costume. The change wasn't only for costumes, Young recalls, but "it made everyone happier."

IDEAS VS REALITY

Which ideas work in motion or onstage? Even experienced artists can't foresee everything prior to having the dancers moving in costume in the space, under lighting. Adjustments happen throughout the process, but even when the performance is close and deadlines are looming, everyone needs to be open to a final evaluation. Part of judging if a costume is "working" is defining what that actually means. Everyone has their own definition of a successful costume, but usually the criteria come in several main categories. Is the costume aesthetically pleasing—does it showcase the movement created by the choreographer and the bodies of the dancers? For most works, the costume is also part of the communication with the audience. If the costumes are not telling the right story or sending the right message, they are not doing their job. Functionality is also a huge issue for dance costumes. If anything about the costume is hindering the dancer's ability to perform the choreography, a conversation needs to happen immediately.

Aesthetics

Do the costumes on stage fulfill the designer's original vision? If they are supposed to seem ethereal, does the fabric float in the air like an after-image of the dancer? Does the style of the costumes align with the lighting, scenery or other stage elements? Or do the costumes seem too soft when compared with the dissonant music and bold slashes of light? And most importantly, do the costumes show the dancers and the choreography to best advantage? Does the focus go to the costume or the wearer? For an artist, the ability to disassociate and evaluate a work objectively comes with experience. No matter how much time or money has been spent, if the designer or the choreographer is not satisfied with a costume, they need to determine what the problem is, and find a way to fix it that is satisfactory to all involved.

Christine Darch at San Francisco Ballet

Sometimes if an element is not right, the best solution is just to eliminate it. Christine Darch worked with her frequent collaborator Dwight Rhoden on a piece for San Francisco Ballet. "He wanted a tutu but very contemporary—it had to be something unusual. [They decided to] make it square, one layer and sheer." For reasons out of her control, the choreographer only worked with the tutus during the final week of rehearsal rather than developing the work with them in mind. And so, unsurprisingly to the experienced designer, "after the first dress, he [Rhoden] and Helgi [Tomasson, the artistic director] agreed that although the tutus were beautiful and interesting, they weren't really serving the work." Luckily, the original plan had been for the dancers to wear the tutus only part of the time, and the leotards they wore underneath were designed to be seen on their own as well as under the skirts. And so, they were able to eliminate the square tutus without having to make any other changes.

Holly Hynes—*Daphnis et Chloé* by Benjamin Millepied at Paris Opera Ballet (Premiere 2014)

Prolific costume designer Holly Hynes was brought to Paris to do *Daphnis et Chloé* at Paris Opera Ballet with choreographer Benjamin Millepied. "I designed it with a contemporary edge but also sort of Grecian," Hynes stated. Her long experience told her to keep the costumes very simple, as the set design by French artist Daniel Buren was a collage of bold colors and patterns. Buren's design used large colorful shapes edged in his signature black and white stripes. The squares and circles were suspended in a variety of overlapping groupings as a backdrop. To keep the focus on the choreography, Hynes designed costumes in solid white for some characters, solid black for others, in a luxuriously fluid silk crepe fabric. She kept the dancers in the same look throughout the piece until the finale number. At that point, all the dancers switched to the bright tones of the set. The shape and fabric of the costumes were otherwise the same, and each dancer was still a solid block of color, just now in green, yellow, blue or orange.

As sometimes happens, once everything was onstage together people thought of new ideas. The artist Buren suggested to the choreographer that adding geometric shapes to echo the set onto the costumes might be interesting. Hynes did not like the proposal at all, but Millepied was intrigued. Hynes was afraid it would look like patches, as if the costumes were supposed to evoke poor people. "As another artist and a purist, I didn't want those patches. [But] I had to show him physically. And have him see it from a distance." She went to the costume shop and asked them to make sample shapes and add them to some of the costumes. "They don't want to do it—they love the look of the ballet. They are proud of it. And, they can tell that I don't want to do it." However, after discussion with Hynes, the costume shop made some shapes, the designer herself arranged and pinned them, and then they sewed them with a temporary basting stitch. The next day they looked at the sample patches on stage, and the choreographer realized that she was right, the costumes should stay as originally designed. "I played the game, I was a collaborator, but in my heart, I knew I was right."

Communication: Does the Costume Tell the Right Story?

Dancers sometimes portray specific characters, and so the costume needs to help the audience understand their personalities and circumstances. Is the witch evil or just mysterious? Is the young man playful, or is the dancer portraying a child? Is the trio supposed to represent everyday people, or an abstraction? Other times the information is more atmospheric, but just as important. Do the costumes give a dry and dusty feeling? Do the outfits give a sense of otherness without evoking a specific country?

Amy Seiwert—*Traveling Alone* for Colorado Ballet (Premiere 2012)

Amy Seiwert's experience being on the road as a freelance choreographer inspired her to create *Traveling Alone*. She would enjoy her day in rehearsal, but then at her hotel, she often craved a social circle. At a hotel the natural place to find some social interaction is the bar, but people make assumptions about a woman alone. Sometimes she just wanted to experience an event like President Obama's election while part of a group. "There is this vulnerability, an urge to connect with others, feeling like an outsider, but still taking that risk to connect." In her initial conversations with costume designer Christine Darch, they talked about using color to separate one woman from the rest of the dancers, four couples. Seiwert's initial impulse was to put the group in white and the soloist in red. For her, "red was not to be sexual, but about strength and contrast. I wanted a strong contrast but didn't want black and white." Darch felt that red seemed too obvious, and also might look too similar to another piece in the program at Colorado Ballet. Darch suggested green. However, when they saw the piece on stage, Seiwert did not like how the green dress looked under the lights, and the overall effect it had on the dance. It did not convey the strength that she wanted. Seiwert noted that Darch "was my hero in that moment . . . Within 24 hours she had made a different costume. In red. It had this weird geometric tutu on it, and she found red and white vinyl in Denver on zero notice." The

choreographer concluded, "It made it such a stronger piece . . . The obvious choice is not always the wrong one."

Karen Young—*Torrent* by Brian Brooks for the Moving Company (Premiere 2013)

A choreographer may choose to completely change the costume look, or other design elements, when a piece is remounted. In most cases, they begin the new version with this intent already, but when designer Karen Young worked with her frequent collaborator Brian Brooks, the decision to shift tones came to them later. Brooks' piece *Torrent* was originally created for student dancers at Juilliard. The original version was a cast of around 30, with the ensemble wearing street clothes in a variety of colors, patterns and shapes. When Young was brought in to work with Brooks on a remount of the work for his own dance company, a group of only eight, his original intent was to preserve the same kind of look. Young put together a variety of street clothes for the piece and they looked at it during a showing. Designer and choreographer were both surprised to realize that the piece was not being well-served anymore. Although Brooks had been happy with the costumes for the piece at Juilliard, and street clothes are a type of aesthetic he commonly likes, Young explained that "it was distracting to see the individual outfits and we lost the choreography. We became distracted looking at each person instead of it being a whole."

Young looked to the music to lead her to a new solution. "There was a lot of repetition and pattern, like Philip Glass music." She used a more unified, neutral color palette: "a spring palette with a lightness to it." And, she unified the clothing shapes as well, "like a flowing skirt or a short drapey top, a loose sort of shirt for the guys. Having a simple clear aesthetic for the clothes that matched the aesthetic of the piece totally transformed the piece." Young felt that with the new costume look, the overall meaning of the work changed. The piece shifted from telling the story of relationships between individuals in an urban setting to "looking just at choreography."

Functionality

Clearly, one of the most important reasons to adjust a costume is if it hinders the dancer's ability to perform in any way. Experience teaches both designers and choreographers to be on the lookout for common pitfalls: hemlines that can cause tripping, sleeves too constricting for full movement, slippery fabrics or dimensional embellishments where a dancer needs to be grabbed by another for partnering. However, seemingly restrictive garments can be completely functional if built correctly and if the movement is in sync with what the costume allows. Ballerinas have been performing in bodices that are basically corsets for centuries, and men dance in off-the-rack non-stretch pants in both musicals and dance pieces regularly. However, if a garment seems to be causing a problem, that doesn't always mean the costume needs to be changed. Dancers are very skilled at movement, and they can often adapt. Sometimes they just need some more time to get used to how a skirt spirals around their legs when they finish a turn, or to subtly shift how they tilt their head as they roll on the floor to accommodate a hat.

With unusual costumes, functionality is harder to predict, and prototypes become all the more important. Heavy items must be centered so that a dancer can keep their balance. A heavy skirt with a hi-low hemline can make *pirouettes* difficult. Hats and headpieces need to be well secured—a chin-strap might hold up for normal movement, but when the dancer bends forward with great velocity, the hat flies right off. A shirt loose enough to allow the dancer to raise her arms in the fitting room might stick to the ribcage once saturated with perspiration.

E. Shura Pollatsek—*The Tortoise and the Hare* by Meghen McKinley and Kylene Stephens for WKU Dance Company (Premiere 2019)

Choreographers Meghen McKinley and Kylene Stephens teamed up for a contemporary dance version of the story *The Tortoise and the Hare*. While they wanted the animal costumes to be evocative, not realistic, they did want the tortoise to have a dome-shaped shell, and the hare to have ears. I knew that before designing the exact shape of the shell, we would have to give the dancer something to rehearse with early in the process and see what she could handle. But since our shop did not have the resources to spend too much time on prototypes, I gave them an existing foam costume from stock to start with, originally ladybug wings, to get some initial feedback. The size seemed about right, but choreographers and designer all agreed the foam needed to be stiffer, to not wrap the dancer like a taco when she rolled. However, I also knew that if the foam was too stiff, it would be unwieldy for the dancer. And so, I had most of the shape of the shell made of a softer seat cushion foam and then we added a thin layer of stiffer floor mat on the side against the dancer's back, to keep it from curving too much. The costume attached like a hiking backpack, with shoulder and waist straps. When the dancer tried it in rehearsal, the choreographers

liked the way it didn't completely hinder her movement but did give her some turtle-like awkwardness. While there was no danger of her actually getting stuck on her back, the audience could believe it might be possible. But they found in rehearsal that later in the dance, when the hare had to wrap her arms around the tortoise from behind, the stiffness together with the width of the shell made that movement impossible. To solve this, we kept the size of the shell unchanged but cut away the outer few inches of the stiff layer just at the sides, and it was enough. I waited until the shape was finalized before I had the shop work on coloring and painting the designs of the shell onto the fabric covering. In this case, form absolutely followed function.

ADJUSTMENTS FOR REVIVALS OR TOURS

Adjustments to costumes for revivals or tours most typically involve altering existing costumes to fit different dancers. If the originals can't fit, aren't available or are too worn out or aged to be reused then new items are built or shopped that fulfill the original design. If a different company hires the choreographer to re-set existing choreography, most typically the choreographer will want to use the same costume design from the original, but the company will produce their own clothing pieces. They will build or shop a new set but will keep the original look as much as possible. Changes should be made in consultation with the original costume designer or their designated design consultant. A common change is using slightly different fabrics. If the original lace can't be found, the best substitution would be a lace that has a different type of floral design up close, but from a distance has the same degree of transparency and similar stiffness. If a dancer with a different body type is featured in a role, the cut of the costume might be adjusted to better suit her. A loose backless dress might be made tighter for a curvy dancer to allow bust support to be built in, for example. Or decoration might be simplified for a shorter dancer so the original amount of detail would not feel crammed in.

Christopher K. Morgan—*Limited Visibility* for Christopher K. Morgan and Artists (Premiere 2012)

The design of a piece might be varied to suit the physical bodies of different dancers, but for certain types of works, both the design and choreography adjust to the performers. Christopher K. Morgan restaged his 2012 work *Limited Visibility* in 2015 with a different cast. The work was about "a sense of evolution and intimacy and creating small spaces where there were solo moments when each dancer revealed something about themselves." Since the dancers' personal experiences became a part of the work, the content and the choreography shifted with the new cast. While the costumes remained black pedestrian clothing, Morgan varied details of the costume to suit the stories of the dancers (he did not work with a costume designer for this piece). The dancers had an additional effect on the design of the piece, as they themselves manipulated the lighting. The lighting, which ranged from paper lanterns to swinging work lights, created intimacy and small spaces in the work. One of the women from the original cast developed a solo with Morgan about hiding herself, "so she ended up in more layers—a drapier layered top that hid her body more. Interestingly, the woman who went into the same role in the remount, her solo also played with hiding. But she was more about 'I had been hiding and now I'm revealing myself' so she had a much more fitted costume." The change in costume also affected the wider look of the piece. The lighting used during this solo created a lot of shadow and silhouette. As the light shone on the original dancer's flowing top, the fabric was not substantial enough to create a distinctly shaped shadow, so instead the viewer's focus was pulled to the clearer shapes of the silhouettes of her head and hands. However, the replacement dancer in her more fitted clothing cast a clear shadow of the whole body on the back wall.

Jody Sperling—*Arctic Memory* (Premiere 2014)

Sometimes, the choreography, not the costume, is what changes for a revival. Jody Sperling created *Arctic Memory* as a solo for herself to dance on location in the Arctic, on the ice, when she went as part of a scientific exhibition (for more on this, see Case Study #5). The costume she danced in was a voluminous hand-painted silk cape, designed to look like the pack ice of the Arctic. Upon her return to New York, she wanted both the costume and the work to "have this other life." She looked for a way to present the costume being danced in on a sheet of ice besides showing filmed footage from the trip, and she decided to re-set the work on an ice skater. The choreography consists of manipulating the flowing silk in swirling shapes around the body. The skater performed outdoors at Rockefeller Center and Chelsea Piers. She not only had to contend with wind as Sperling did in the Arctic, she also had to contend with the turbulence caused by her actual skating. Because of the wind currents potentially hitting the skater from multiple angles, Sperling had expected to need to drastically alter some of the movements. Instead, she found herself impressed by how much of the original dance the skater was able to preserve, and her changes were much more minor than she had anticipated.

The explorations needed to develop a dance from movement phrases and yards of velvet into an entire piece work best if designers and choreographers stay in constant communication. Once the extensive floorwork section is added in, with newly dissonant music, does head to toe velvet still feel like the right look? Perhaps it should just be an accent. Can those yards of silk velvet that summed up the emotional quality of the dance get thrown in the washer when the company tours overseas? Perhaps stretch velvet could work instead, even if the drape is not as nuanced. Choreographer Kyle Abraham said, "I actually depend on my collaborators to give me thoughts or ideas on what to do or how they see the work. Then I can say 'no that's still not it,' or 'yeah that's awesome.' And then it helps me to actually finish the dance. I can't have a dance finished without having a sense of what the costumes are going to be."

Case Study #6

Appalachian Spring

CHOREOGRAPHER—PAUL VASTERLING

COMPANY—NASHVILLE BALLET

PREMIERE DATE—2017

DATE PHOTOGRAPHED—MARCH 2017

PERFORMANCE VENUE—SCHERMERHORN SYMPHONY CENTER

PREMIERE OF WORK—2016

MUSIC COMPOSITION—AARON COPLAND

MUSIC PERFORMANCE—NASHVILLE SYMPHONY

CONDUCTOR—GIANCARLO GUERRERO

COSTUME DESIGN—HOLLY HYNES

LIGHTING DESIGN—SCOTT LEATHERS

Dancers from Nashville Ballet perform *Appalachian Spring*

Aaron Copeland's beloved work *Appalachian Spring* soars through the concert hall. Much as the strings and winds generate a rich, symphonic version of American folk music, the dancers on the stage in front of them capture the charm and energy of early Americana, but infused with sophisticated lyricism and dramatic leaps. Soft, rustic fabrics form geometric shapes as dancers cluster into a circle or hold their partners aloft.

In his 20 years as Artistic Director for Nashville Ballet, Paul Vasterling has created over 40 works, ranging from classic story ballets like *Peter Pan* to works based on unexpected topics like Tennessee Williams' play *Night of the Iguana*. His work encompasses both classical ballet and contemporary ballet, but "I am really interested in humanity so you're not going to find truly abstract pieces from me, no matter where the needle falls on the level of classicism in it." When Nashville Symphony initiated a collaboration on *Appalachian Spring* between the Symphony and Nashville Ballet, Vasterling jumped at the chance to stage the beautiful Copeland music. He chose his frequent collaborator Holly Hynes for costumes.

Vasterling's first task was to find a new take on the classic by developing choreography that would pay tribute to Martha Graham, but in his own language. Aaron Copland originally composed *Appalachian Spring* in 1944 for choreographer Martha Graham. The evocative music written for a small ensemble used quintessential American styles like fiddle tunes and hymns, including the famous Shaker hymn "Simple Gifts." The setting was a pioneer settlement, which also symbolized the founding spirit of America. Graham's ballet followed a young couple about to be married, with additional characters of a preacher, an older pioneer woman and an ensemble of fellow settlers.

To create his work, Vasterling often weaves together disparate influences—ideas from novels he reads, paintings or historical research. His recent ballet *Lucy Negro, Redux* is based on a book of poetry by fellow Nashvillian Caroline Randall Williams written from the point of view of Shakespeare's "dark lady," subject of many of his sonnets. His *Lizzie Borden* ballet was influenced by a book he happened to read about shadow people, which he imagined to be like ghosts one sees out of the corner of the eye. To create his own *Appalachian Spring*, Vasterling of course started with the music. He studied both the score itself and the historical context of the time it was written. He chose to simplify the storyline from the original and altered the characters to a mother figure and a group of young people. "I started thinking about the Graham version and how the central figures were a man and a woman making their way through

the world and decided to have a more feminist view and make it just about a woman."

As he worked through the themes of the piece, he continued to reflect on the original creators. Vasterling explained how during a conversation with a friend, they realized the irony that this quintessential American work "was written by a group of outsiders: a woman, a gay Jew and a Japanese man in 1944 [Graham, Copeland and artist/set designer Isamu Noguchi] . . . That really set the theme of [my version of] the ballet—a central figure that represents a mother [but also] the idea of America . . . there is opportunity and then there are outsiders, and the outsiders are always trying to get in." This realization helped him find a contemporary connection for the material, not only with immigration but also to a variety of social issues. The premise of outsiders trying to get in drove the work forward. One of the most noticeable uses of the theme stems from the idea of musical chairs. Vasterling incorporated Shaker style chairs in several groupings throughout the piece—in a circle in the center echoing the game of musical chairs, in a wider arc creating an inclusive space, and in a line across the back where dancers sit observing the others.

Although not a practitioner of Graham's technique, Vasterling wanted his expressionistic ballet choreography to pay homage to the modern dance icon. He began choreographing the ballet in his usual style, starting with just the principal dancer. Striving to echo the music, he worked with her to establish the basic vocabulary of the piece before he expanded to the whole group. He describes his choreography for the piece as "contemporary feeling—it has a lot of weight." His usual mode of working is to finish the concept before beginning choreography. "I'm a big planner, so the movements don't drive it, the concept drives it." However, with *Appalachian Spring* he didn't resolve everything until he had worked for a while with the dancers in the studio. His connection to the material deepened, driven by some events happening in his own life. He went from seeing the mother figure as a symbolic idea of America to relating the work to his own family, and the emotional connection helped him resolve the sections into a whole. "I couldn't figure out how to finish this ballet and then suddenly realized it was a tribute to my mother."

Vasterling works with a variety of designers, but he likes Holly Hynes' style for his more minimalistic pieces. Her years of experience designing for top companies around the world including American Ballet Theatre, the Bolshoi Ballet and the Paris Opera Ballet have honed her ability to bring out thematic ideas without

Katie Vasilopoulos as the Mother

Dancer Augusto Cezar

Brett Sjoblom and Cezar as two of the sons.

Cezar and Julia Eisen

overwhelming the expressive power of the dancer's body. "The great thing about Holly is . . . she really understands ballet and movement and . . . she is not pounding you the viewer with her design idea, she is able to let it be part of the whole dance, and understands that her work can either amplify or diminish the main voice, [the body]." As Vasterling's concept developed more layers, and he worked on interweaving the abstract themes of outsider-ness, tradition and his family connection, he confirmed his feeling that she was the right collaborator for this ballet.

Hynes is indeed best known for her streamlined looks and for her connection with dancers. When presenting the 2018 TDF/Irene Sharaff Lifetime Achievement Award in Costume Design, Prima Ballerina Wendy Whelan said Hynes was "truly a dancer's designer." As the Director of Costumes at New York City Ballet for 21 years, Hynes designed more than 70 ballets for the company. She had the opportunity to work with a wide variety of choreographers, and also learned the history of her predecessors as she led the costume shop through accurate reproductions of costumes for original Robbins and Balanchine ballets from the mid-twentieth century.

When developing a work, Hynes and Vasterling not only discuss ideas and look at sketches, but also explore research together in person. For a previous work, *Layla and the Majnun*, they went to

Vasilopoulos with the ensemble. Note she is wearing her shawl look.

Judson Veach airborne as the other dancers watch.

the Islamic Art section of the Metropolitan Museum in New York. They wandered the galleries, responding to artifacts and images and pointing out details to each other. For *Appalachian Spring*, they visited a Shaker village. Hynes studied the colors and textures of Shaker artifacts, as well as the balanced simplicity. The designer was struck by the idea that they are "people of the earth but also of the heavens."

Hynes begins any dance costume design by connecting with the music. She strives to translate not only what the music says to the choreographer, but also what it says to her. "Shutting your eyes and seeing what you imagine as you listen—maybe that morphs or changes [your ideas] or gives you some other new direction." Edithe Gilfond's costume design for the original *Appalachian Spring* featured Graham's signature full skirts, but as part of a realistic, although simplified, translation of Shaker clothing to modern dance. Hynes developed a more pared down look than the original, while keeping to Vasterling's request that the dancers look like individual people in real clothes. Together they created a character for each dancer—the troublesome one, the youngest, the quiet one. After developing shapes for the costumes, she chose earthy textures and colors with an added a touch of stronger hue on each dancer, and also used pattern to create a "relaxed and simple" feeling—plaid skirt panels for the women and striped shirts for the men. Each of the ensemble dancers has a touch of color, while most of the clothing is tones of tan and beige. However, the Mother character's dress is a rich golden hue. While still a natural and earthy ochre, her stronger color pulls the audience's eye, the warmth that binds her family. The Mother's outfit is the most related to Shaker clothing, while Hynes revealed more skin on the younger characters.

To develop this alternate silhouette, Hynes looked to the era of *Appalachian Spring*'s premiere for inspiration, the 1940s. She kept the flavor of Graham's full skirts, but only the Mother has the long, covering length. She designed a skirt shape with inset panels that open and close like a fan as the dancer turns; the touch of colorful plaid gives a bit of a surprise for the audience. Hynes describes her connection with Graham's work being that she "didn't want to lose the heaviness and the flow of the skirt . . . because it takes so long for that big old skirt to come back to earth." Due to the

ballet's schedule, the costume designs had to be well underway before Hynes could see the full company in rehearsal. However, they made a prototype skirt that Vasterling was able to work with on the principal dancer in his early rehearsals. The weight and flow of the skirt influenced Vasterling's choreography, and he developed the movement with Hynes' designs in mind, knowing that, as he described, "It's not just what [the skirt] can do, it's what it masks. The leg work becomes less significant. In ballet—classical or even neoclassical—we speak so much with the legs. So, this makes it a little more contemporary because it focuses the movement up to the torso and the arms."

Hynes made sure that the period flavor of the piece did not overwhelm the primary objective—showing the lines of the dancers' bodies and the subtleties of the choreography. The men's costumes have the V neckline of a vest, but the designer skips the expected shirt collar in order to showcase collarbone and neck. The pants look like pants not tights, but they are cut fairly lean so that the shapes of the legs are still clearly apparent. The younger women's halter-shaped bodice cuts a flattering diagonal across the torso and shows the shoulders to advantage. Hynes' fabric choices captured exactly what Vasterling was looking for and were in harmony with the score. He appreciated that the men's sleeves had movement to them, "kind of like the music, it has this ecstatic wave to it." The total stage picture has simplicity but also texture, pathos and joy.

Although the Mother's costume stayed more covering than the rest of the cast, Hynes streamlined her design from her original concept after seeing the piece in rehearsal. Based on her vast experience, she knew that it was "better to have it all and then take it away than to get on stage and think 'that's not enough.' Because then you're [creating new garments] at the last minute and it's not your best work." Designer and choreographer decided that a narrower sleeve would better show the lines of the dancer's body in her solo work, and the shawl and head covering should only be worn during part of the dance. Successful designers like Hynes not only plan for but embrace the constant change that comes with live performance. "Every time I watch [a piece] I see something different I hadn't seen before. And that's just thrilling. That's a living piece of art."

Vasilopoulos and ensemble dancers with Nashville Symphony in the background

6

The Process—Finishing: Declaring a Final Product and Beyond

RECOGNIZING A SUCCESSFUL DESIGN

While designers and choreographers have varying ideas about the aesthetics of costumes and how best to approach the design process, they are surprisingly aligned when it comes to judging a success. Good designs become an essential part of the work. As costume designer Sandra Woodall put it, "Everything should be so interwoven that you wouldn't imagine another choice." Designs that don't work distract from the movement, rather than complementing it. Designer Branimira Ivanova noted that "in dance reviews you don't get kudos for costumes. They only notice them if they are bad. Which means that if they don't say anything about them it doesn't mean that they were not noticeable, but that they were so integral that they were part of it, they were completing it." Designer Christine Darch agreed. "A costume should enhance and support and enable, perhaps punctuate, the movement but not be the most present thing on stage." Liz Vandal feels that design enhances a dance by helping to transmit its message, and even abstract works tell a kind of story. "A successful design is a design that serves a purpose. . . . I realized [during my career] that it's all in the way we tell the story first, to ourselves. And the feeling that we have when it's on stage—we say 'wow' not only because it's beautiful, but because it's meaningful . . . It all has to do with a certain kind of purity, that it's one with the body, that it's one

Nile Alicia Ruff and Quentin ApolloVaughn Sledge of Dayton Contemporary Dance perform *This I Know for Sure* by Ray Mercer, costume design by Elena Comendador

Dancers Bridge Taylor, Julia Mitchell and Brett Sjoblom from Nashville Ballet perform *The Four Seasons* by Paul Vasterling, costumes by David Heuvel

being. We don't want to hear, 'oh she is wearing a nice skirt.' You don't see the costume; you see the grace of the dancer."

A successful design comes from a collaboration where all the artists involved feel like they can explore, so the product becomes more than the sum of its parts. Nicole Haskins complimented her design collaborator by noting "in what she did I saw things that I had never imagined, but had been my intention." Choreographer Jack Ferver summed up his collaborations with Reid Bartelme: "I said the idea I had, and then he made something better than what I had said." Ferver relies on designers for their expertise, knowing that dancers might not have the capacity to rein in their impulses and ensure a look is effective. "We are visual, and dance is a visual thing. I always tell my students that . . . just because it feels good doesn't mean it looks good." Choreographer Septime Webre believes costume design can "elevate the dance, not just complement it. It brings something extra that elevates the whole proceeding. But it can't overtake the dance, it must support the movement. It's got to understand how the body moves, how the body is complemented."

Choreographer Amy Seiwert wants all of her collaborators to stretch themselves during the creation of a piece. "What I like to think I have is a real relationship of trust with the dancers I work with. The creation process is so vulnerable for all of us, on every side. I will often ask dancers to be uncomfortable creatively. . . . I will often push them to places that might feel unfamiliar . . . With trust, we will get to more interesting places. I like to think that holds true with costuming too." Costume designer John Ahrens has a similar philosophy. He not only wants to execute designs; he also wants to be stretched artistically. "What works best for me is to form a relationship with a choreographer that challenges both of us."

SHOULD AN ARTIST HAVE A STYLE?

While most artists do not actively seek to develop a style, over time their body of work shows their strengths and their taste. And so, choosing collaborators affects the form of the finished work—the gumbo created by the members of the creative team takes on the flavors of the components put in. Liz Vandal explained how she chose her own brand. "Even if we are very versatile, our signature or our spirit shows through. The name I chose, Vandal, has to do with that: angular, warrior like, very strong. Even if I do soft, it's powerful." Melanie Watnick finds it helpful to study a choreographer's style when they collaborate. "Each choreographer has their own movement vocabulary. I try to think of adjectives that describe their movement like fluid, sinewy, angular, vibrant. The

more I work with that choreographer, the more I understand what their movement is."

Karen Young described her career's path. "I got more into doing costumes that feel like clothes. Not pedestrian but relating more to fashion and streetwear than to dancewear. That's what people come to me for. I am good at making anything work for dance, making anything work for movement." The duo Reid & Harriet Design think that their training is the origin of their style. Reid Bartelme believes that "one of the really important things in our work is that there be a directness to it. We like to make whatever point we are trying to make in the most direct way possible." His co-designer Harriet Jung added "when you hear 'costume design' there is a very specific idea of what that is—very theater-oriented and also more conservative. What Reid and I have because of our fashion design background is a little fresher in terms of our designs for dance. I think that's what makes us a little different than most costume designers." But she does not think designers should be too wedded to a certain style. "If it serves the piece, we will do things that are not totally characteristic of us but still do it in a way that is Reid & Harriet."

THE LONG VIEW

Again, although the artists interviewed for this book range widely in aesthetic and method, they also have absorbed similar lessons during their careers. Not surprising for those who work in a collaborative art form, most learned how to step back from their own egos and be more receptive to the group. Jack Ferver knows where his strengths lie. "I am clear in my vision, but I let my collaborators do what they are better at than me." Experienced artists know when to let go, and that adapting their ideas is part of the journey, not a setback. Christine Darch said "I think that when you collaborate, you have to understand that nothing can be precious. If they cut something, then every new choice you make is [another] opportunity to do something that you like to design."

Designers and choreographers both also have learned how to simplify, and to get out of their own way. David Heuvel knows that "no matter how complicated it is, it's about the dance, the steps and the movement, and the costumes have to complement that and not intrude. In my early days it was all about the costume for me, rather than what the choreographer was intending. I had a tendency in the beginning to over-design—I wanted it all on that one costume. But you can do a third of that and it will still be too much. Make it as simple and as beautiful as you can." While Jack Ferver currently relies on striking design visuals to complete his

Dancers from Dayton Contemporary Dance Company perform *Beyond a Cliff* by Dwight Rhoden costumes by L'Amour

performance pieces, his early work was very simple. He figured out his own illumination with clip lights and used costumes from the dancers' closets. This foundation "kept me focused on the work and what it really needs: connection with the audience." Now he tells young people: "If you feel this need to pile on a lot, and have a lot, it means that you don't know what you are saying. I love hyperbole, and I use it a lot, but I edit. A lot. Because the work isn't for me, it's for an audience."

Many established artists have learned how to either subtly or overtly teach their methods of collaboration to less experienced colleagues. Emily Morgan was surprised by a choreographer who complimented her on opening night by remarking how wonderful it was that the costume designer was so invested in her piece. Morgan replied, "well, it's my piece too." The designer feels that if she "puts in the time to establish what a good working relationship can be" with young choreographers, she pays it forward by helping them to collaborate in the future with other designers. Over time she learned how to balance confidence with openness, and advocate for her own ideas without being defensive. She learned to ask questions but bring ideas to the table too. Holly Hynes voiced a similar philosophy. "You are not just one artist in a room. Listen, share your opinions too, but take note of what the group has to say. It might be the lighting designer, the wardrobe mistress, it might be the assistant to the choreographer, listen to everybody. The bottom line is you all want this to be a special production and the fun is collaborating and learning from each other."

There is no right way to create art or to collaborate. But overall, to create successful costumes for dance, choreographers and designers need to have a clear roadmap for how they will approach their journey, and when the route becomes unpredictable, good communication to get back on track. Any artist can broaden their range of methods, and learn to be creative with their creative process as well as with the inspiration and the outcome. With practice, designers and choreographers can experiment together and investigate new pathways in an increasingly productive and satisfying fashion.

Choreographers are used to exploring alongside dancers, whether they actually use the dancers as co-creators, or just to try out movement phrases in the studio. Choreographers may use preexisting music and create to that, or they might create movement first and then find or even commission music to go with it. They should feel they can try these same kinds of options with costume design. Likewise, designers need to understand how to create innovative looks, but also work with choreographers and dancers to ensure that new ideas have a chance to be fully understood, tested and adapted.

Both designers and choreographers will be well served if they periodically focus on and improve their ability to be creative. Both sides can get bogged down in technique—landing the perfect double *pirouette*, creating a graphic print that that will not fade in the wash, figuring out how to gracefully unfasten and remove a skirt on stage. All artists need to remember that while these techniques enhance a work, they are the means not the end. Any component needs to serve the overall work. A beautiful leg extension may not convey the right quality of movement for a low grounded section. A pair of pants might be finely tailored, but too pedestrian for an abstract work. Dialog with other artists serves to keep the goals of a work fresh.

Dancers from Contra-Tiempo perform *joyUs justUS* by Ana Maria Alvarez

Appendix

As a college student working on my first dance design, I thought I was being clever by buying cheap, floaty ponytail scarves and making them into skirts for the ten dancers. But the scarves were too lightweight, and the points weren't staying down, so I sewed buttons to each of the points. We gave them a first try in the studio. The dancers came to a section of the choreography when they rolled on the floor, and we were serenaded by the clickety click clink of all the buttons hitting the floor. Needless to say, I then had to take off those 30 buttons that I had so carefully sewed on.

I have come a long way since then. Here are some tips and tricks I've learned over the years that I'm sharing with you.

PLANNING THE COSTUME

Questions for costume designers to ask/specifics for choreographers to make clear:

- What is the cast size?
- Groupings—are there large groups? Duets, trios or solos mixed into the work?
- Is the work divided into sections or movements?
- Do dancers follow specific gender roles? Should the costumes be ungendered?
- Should the costumes be matching, variations on a theme, or should everyone be different?
- Are the dancers abstract beings? People? Characters?
- Is there floor work? Is there partnering, and how close is the contact? Do they go upside-down? Are other unusual movements planned?
- Who touches who where and how?
- Are there sub-groups to define?

- Are the dancers' roles designated by importance? (Standard ballet terms for this are principal/soloist/corps.)
- Do the dancers stay in a specific order or spacing onstage? (This can be helpful to decide how to distribute colors, etc.) Even if it's not always the same, is there a particular arrangement to highlight or use as a baseline?
- Are there costume changes during the piece? If so, how long do dancers have to change?
- What is the performance space like? What is the floor like? Where is the audience?
- What kind of footwear do the dancers need? Or will they be barefoot?
- Does the work have a planned mood or style?
- What genre of dance is it? (Ballet, modern jazz, postmodern, hip hop etc.)
- Does the choreographer have any initial visual images? Do they see a certain color? A type of fabric or garment?
- Do they plan to use double casting of roles? Do they have understudies?

Which visuals are the choreographer's decision?

- In dance, choreographers usually have the primary say over shoes, socks and tights.
- For ballet, choreographers usually specify skirt type, and whether men are in tights or pants.
- In traditional ballet, shoes match tights unless the choreographer says differently.
- For any genre, choreographers often specify skirts vs pants vs shorts.
- For a group piece, they may want to decide if skirt or pant hems are proportional to the dancer's body, the same distance off the floor, or all actually the same length.

Special logistical needs to plan for:

- Touring
- How and where will the costumes be stored?
- Are there unusual elements like water onstage, an outdoor performance, etc.?

Guidelines for undergarments:

- If undergarments are needed, consider if they should be skin-toned garments or purposely not skin-toned. (Especially in terms of briefs or shorts, what do you want the audience to imagine they are seeing if they see the undergarment? Clothing or skin?)
- What is the main purpose of the undergarment? Modesty? Sweat absorption?
- Is uniformity important, or can each dancer wear what they prefer or what suits them best?
- Do dancers want bust or other body support and if so what kind? Do they need to wear knee braces or other supportive devices?
- Bike shorts or tights underneath a garment help combat "camel toe."

IMPLEMENTING THE DESIGN

Always assume everyone needs the full range of movement unless told otherwise—everyone needs to kick their leg up to their head, be able to do a deep *plié* in second (the best test for whether a crotch sits high enough in pants), they will all roll on the floor.

Tips for choosing pedestrian clothes that work for dance:

- Full skirts flow better if flared or A-line not dirndl or rectangular.
- Select pants with stretch if at all possible if they are slim cut. If there will be much floor work, be sure the fabric is sturdy enough to not wear through knees, etc.
- For stretch garments, especially ones not built as dance or athletic clothing, be sure the stretch has a lot of elasticity and springs back firmly. Leggings with stretched-out knees are not pretty.
- Consider sweat absorption—beware of thin fabrics especially on tighter clothing. Also, some colors will show sweat more, especially with cotton.
- Consider if they can be laundered, or other maintenance issues like how much ironing will be required.

Adapting clothes to work better for dance:

- Add gussets (football-shaped fabric insets) to crotches and armholes for more movement.
- For a better range of motion in fitted garments, the crotch needs to sit high, also armholes on a sleeved garment.
- Add in stretch panels to seams or other inconspicuous places or make them a feature.
- To keep shoulder straps from falling off shoulders, angle them so they are closer to center either in the front or the back.
- Make sure pant-waists are snug so they don't stretch out and slide down when dancers get sweaty. If fabric is quite stretchy, reinforce the waist with firmer elastic either inside or outside as a belt. You don't want it so tight it cuts into them, but it needs to stay up.
- Skin-toned mesh is your friend! It's more invisible in most lighting than "clear" straps and can help to support and smooth a lot of oddly shaped necklines and support decoration.
- If there is a lot of floor work, replace buttons or other bumpy closures with something flatter or softer.

Choosing fabrics and clothing for dyeing:

- Know which fibers take dye well. Polyester is not your friend, although it's possible.
- Buy extra yardage for samples, or an extra garment for tests.
- Plan for shrinkage in a hot dye bath, especially in the length of garments.
- Even the same brand of dancewear might take dye differently from one garment to another, as the fabrics may be slightly different even if made of the same fiber. It's better to make shorts and a tank out of unitards then to try to dye two different garments the exact same color.
- Sometimes it's easier to buy a garment and dye it, sometimes dyeing a specific shade can be difficult enough it's actually easier to make something out of the right color fabric, and it's more colorfast for laundry.

Dance-friendly structure:

- If things need structure, better that it can collapse and spring back than get dented (plastic or foam, not wire).
- Plastic boning, foam, nylon horsehair, plastic needlepoint canvas can all be used to stiffen but also not hurt dancers or get in the way if they roll, etc.

- Check decoration and textured fabrics to be sure any texture doesn't grab onto the dancer's own costume or that of other dancers. Rhinestones, sequins and things like that can get caught, especially in meshy fabrics. You can't always foresee if someone's ankle will be near someone else's shoulder or not.
- Consider placement of any dimensional decoration for partnering and grabbing.

Creating a successful prototype:

- Be sure it moves and behaves like the real thing—how it functions is at least as important as how it looks. If possible, use the actual real fabric for a rehearsal garment.

Tips for fittings:

- Have them move! The dancer can go out in the hallway and do a cartwheel if you need to. But they should just mark through the dance if they are not warmed up.
- Mark placement of decoration while it's on the dancer's body, especially on stretch garments.
- Attach anything non-stretch to something stretch while it's on the body if at all possible. (like non-stretch trim along the neckline of a leotard, for example) The exact degree of stretch needed is hard to predict and if it's too stretched it will look rippled, if it's too tight it won't fit.

FIXING LOGISTICAL ISSUES

Making it stay on and stay in place:

- Elastic loops on shirt side-seams that attach to buttons on pants waistband hold an untucked shirt down but still allow movement. These are often called ballet loops.
- If chin-straps do not hold well enough try Y-straps like a bike helmet.
- Add skin-toned finger loops on long sleeves if they ride up.
- Add elastic into hems on garments like leggings. Always fit the elastic loop for the hem around the dancer's leg or arm to be sure it's tight enough but not too tight, and ideally not placed at the widest point on the musculature, like the widest part of the thigh, or it will want to ride up.
- Picking the right elastic is important—what width, how much elasticity, do you need rubber grips, etc.
- Skin-toned mesh!
- Attach things to trunks if needed (skirts to keep from rotating, shirts to keep them down, etc.).
- Tack ballet bodices to ballet skirts to keep them down. Actually sew them, by hand, for the run of the show.
- Tack classical tutus with a tagging gun to save time, rather than hand-sewing. This can be to tack the layers together, or to tack a decorative skirt to a preexisting tutu structure.

Index

Note: The Index uses US spelling. Page numbers in **bold** refer to photographs.